POEMS OF

HEINRICH HEINE

Illustrated by *Fritz Kredel*

POEMS OF

HEINRICH HEINE

Selected and Translated, with an Introduction, by

LOUIS UNTERMEYER

and Illustrated by

FRITZ KREDEL

THE HERITAGE PRESS

NEW YORK

C O N T E N T S

~~~~~~~~~~~~~~~~~~~~~~~~~~

AN INTRODUCTION   *xix*

YOUTHFUL SORROWS

PREFACE TO THE "BOOK OF SONGS"   *3*
TWO DREAM SONNETS   *6*
   I dreamed I saw myself puffed up with pride   *6*
   I dreamed I saw a dwarf in dapper clothing   *6*
SONGS   *7*
   Lonely now, I pour my sadness   *7*
   When I am with my own adored   *9*
   Mornings I arise and wonder   *9*
   It drives me here, it drives me there   *10*
   Wandering under dark branches   *11*
   My love, lay your hand on my heart in its gloom *12*
   I wish that all my love-songs   *12*
   Lovely cradle of my sorrow   *13*

CONTENTS

Hill and hall are mirrored brightly   *14*
I despaired at first, declaring   *15*
With rose and with cypress, with tinsel and gold   *15*
When young hearts break with passion   *16*
There's green on meadow and river   *17*
I thought about her all the day   *18*
I love you, little Mopser   *19*
Certainly the advice was good   *20*
You were a maiden, blonde, without a flaw   *20*

NARRATIVES

POOR PETER   *22*
  Oh, Hansel and Gretel are dancing around   *22*
  "Within my breast there's such a woe"   *23*
  Poor Peter, he goes stumbling by   *23*
THE PRISONER'S SONG   *24*
THE MESSAGE   *25*
THE GRENADIERS   *26*
BELSHAZZAR   *28*
THE MINNESINGERS   *30*
THE WOUNDED KNIGHT   *31*
DIALOG ON PADERBORN HEATH   *32*
ABSOLUTELY!   *34*
SONNET TO MY MOTHER   *34*

CONTENTS

LYRICAL INTERMEZZO

All my anguish, all my rages	*36*
There once was a knight full of sorrow and doubt	*36*
In May, the magic month of May	*39*
Out of my tears and sorrows	*40*
The rose and the lily, the dove and the sun	*40*
Whene'er I look into your eyes	*40*
Your face has grown so dear, it seems	*41*
Oh, lean your cheek against my cheek	*41*
I will baptize my spirit	*42*
Immovable for ages	*42*
On wings of song, my dearest	*43*
The lotus-blossom cowers	*44*
In the Rhine, that stream of wonder	*44*
You love me not, you love me not	*45*
O come, love, now I resign me	*45*
O kiss me, love, and never swear	*46*
Upon my dearest's little eyes	*46*
The world is dull, the world is blind	*47*
Come, and you shall tell me, dearest	*47*
Like the Foam-born, my love glows in	*48*
I will not mourn, although my heart is torn	*49*
Yes, you are wretched, and I do not mourn	*49*
The violins are shrilling	*50*
So now you have forgotten wholly	*50*
And were it known to the flowers	*51*
Oh, why are all the roses so pale	*51*
They have told you many stories	*52*
The linden blossomed, the nightingale sang	*53*

CONTENTS

How deep we were wrapped in each other's life   53
I have no faith in Heaven   54
You were steadfast and true the longest   55
The earth kept hoarding up its treasure   55
And thus, as I wasted many a day   56
The violets blue which are her eyes   56
The world is so fair and the heaven so blue   57
Love, when you sink where darkness lies   57
A lonely pine is standing   58
Stars, with fair and golden ray   58
Oh, were I but the stool that she   59
Oh, were I but the cushion, too   59
Oh, were I but the least—the mere   59
Since, my love, we had to part   59
From my great grief, I fashion   60
It will not die, but solely   60
Smug burghers and tradesmen are tripping   61
From graves of times forgotten   62
A young man loves a maiden   63
Friendship, Love, the Philosopher's Stone   64
I hear an echo singing   64
Now all the flowers are gazing   65
I dreamed of the daughter of a king   65
My dearest, we nestled devoted   66
From ancient fairy-stories   66
I loved thee once, and I love thee now   67
On a radiant summer morning   68
My love and its dark magic   68
Many have made me wretched   69
The golden flame of summer   69

CONTENTS

When two who love are parted 70

'Twas tea-time; the mildly aesthetic 70

My songs, you say, are poisoned 71

Again the old dream came to me 72

I stand on the mountain's summit 72

My carriage rolls on slowly 73

I wept as I lay dreaming 74

Belovèd, in dreams we often meet 75

A howling storm is brewing 75

Wild autumn shakes the branches 76

A star, a star is falling 77

The Dream-God led me to a castle grim 77

'Twas midnight, still and very cold 78

They buried him at the cross-roads 79

Now the night grows deeper, stronger 80

Night lay upon my eyelids 80

The songs so old and bitter 82

THE HOME-COMING

In my life's too constant darkness 84

I cannot tell why this imagined 85

My heart is full of sorrow 86

I pace the greenwood, bitter 88

The night is wet and stormy 88

By chance I met on the journey 89

We sat by the hut of the fisher 91

Oh, lovely fishermaiden 92

The yellow moon has risen 93

CONTENTS

The moon is lying on the clouds	*93*
Wrapped in clouds, as in a mantle	*94*
The wind pulls up his water-spouts	*95*
The storm tunes up for dancing	*96*
Over the sea's vast acres	*96*
I pass your little dwelling	*98*
The vastness of the ocean shone	*99*
High up on yonder mountain	*99*
My sweetheart has a lily	*100*
Wrapped in the distant sunset	*101*
Greetings to you, great city	*101*
To old paths and familiar streets	*102*
I stood as in a spell	*102*
The night is still; the streets are quiet	*103*
How can you sleep so soundly	*104*
A maiden lies in her chamber	*104*
I stood bewildered, seeing	*105*
I, unfortunate Atlas! A whole world	*106*
The years keep coming and going	*106*
I dreamed: The moon shone sadly down	*107*
Why does this lonely tear-drop	*107*
The pale, autumnal half-moon	*108*
Well, this is awful weather	*110*
They think that I am tortured	*110*
Oh, your slim, white lily-fingers	*111*
"Has she never even shown you"	*112*
They loved one another, though neither	*112*
When I told of my sorrows that wounded and tore	*113*
I called the devil and he came	*113*
Mortal, mock not at the devil	*114*

CONTENTS

Three holy kings from the Orient 115
My child, we once were children 115
My heart is crushed with grief, for sadly 117
As the moon through heavy cloud-drifts 117
I saw in a dream the belovèd 118
"Why, my friend, this same old fretting" 119
Listen, do not grow impatient 120
Now it is time that I should start 120
The good king Wiswamitra 121
Heart, my heart, let naught o'ercome you 121
Child, you are like a flower 122
Child, I know 'twould be your ruin, 122
When I lie down for comfort 123
Girl, whose mouth is red and laughing 123
Snows and storms may whirl in torrents 124
Mary's praise is never done 125
Did not my pallid face betray 125
"Ah, my friend, you are in love" 126
I sought your side, the only 126
Sapphires are those eyes of yours 127
I have lied to win you, precious 128
Life in this world is a muddled existence 128
My head and brain are almost broken 128
They're having a party this evening 129
Oh, could I capture my sadness 129
You've pearls and you've diamonds, my dearest 130
He who, for the first time, loves 131
In your tepid soul and vapid 131
Oh, loveliest of ladies, may 132
Of words and advice they were the donors 132

CONTENTS

This most amiable youngster   *133*

I dreamt I was the dear Lord God   *134*

Torn from bright lips I loved; departing sadly   *136*

It was in July that I lost you   *137*

Alone in the darkened post-chaise   *137*

Like a dark dream the houses   *138*

God knows where I'll find that silly   *139*

With kisses my lips were wounded by you   *139*

And when you're once my wedded wife   *140*

When I am wrapped in her tender embraces   *140*

Oh, what lies there are in kisses   *140*

Upon your snow-white shoulder   *141*

The blue Hussars go bugling   *142*

In my youth when love was yearning   *143*

Have you really grown to hate me   *143*

Ah, these eyes again which always   *144*

'Tis a heavenly pleasure indeed   *144*

Don't shame me, darling; keep your place   *145*

Yes, friend, here Unter den Linden   *145*

Hard to understand your gabble   *146*

And still the eunuchs grumbled   *146*

On the walls of Salamanca   *147*

As soon as we met we were wrapt in each other   *147*

Over the mountains the sun throws his fire   *148*

In Halle's market-place   *148*

Lovely and efficient lady   *149*

Night lies on the strange, dark roadways   *150*

Death, it is but the long, cool night   *150*

Softly now the summer twilight   *151*

"Where now is your precious darling"   *152*

CONTENTS

TALES AND IDYLS

DONNA CLARA *153*
THE PILGRIMAGE TO KEVLAAR *158*
  The mother stood at the window *158*
  The Mother of God in Kevlaar *159*
  The heartsick son and his mother *161*
PROLOG TO "THE HARZ JOURNEY" *162*
MOUNTAIN IDYL *163*
  On the mountain stands a cabin *163*
  Now the fir-tree's long, green fingers *165*
  Still the bashful moon is hiding *168*
THE HERD-BOY *172*
ON THE BROCKEN *173*
ILSE *174*

FROM "THE NORTH SEA"

CORONATION *176*
TWILIGHT *178*
NIGHT ON THE STRAND *179*
THE SEA HAS ITS PEARLS *182*

NEW SPRING

SONGS *183*
  Here's May again, with its lifting *183*
  Lightly swinging bells are ringing *184*

CONTENTS

The butterfly is in love with the rose   *185*
All the trees are full of music   *185*
"In the beginning was the word"   *186*
I must go forth, the bells are pealing   *187*
Ah, I long for tears returning   *188*
The slender water-lily   *188*
What drives you out in this night of spring   *189*
Your eyes' blue depths are lifted   *189*
I wander where budding bowers   *190*
Come, tell me whose super-intelligent power   *190*
There was an agèd monarch   *191*
In memory many pictures   *192*
Every morn I send you violets   *192*
Your letter does not move me   *193*
Stars with golden feet are walking   *193*
The sweet desires blossom   *194*
Autumn mists, cold dreams are filling   *194*

A GARLAND OF GIRLS

SERAPHINE   *195*
Through the dusky wood I wander   *195*
Night has come with silent footsteps   *196*
How this too anxious sea-gull   *196*
Shadow-love and shadow-kisses   *197*
Upon the shore, a maiden   *198*
I've told no man how shameful   *199*
ANGELIQUE   *199*
Although you hurried coldly past me   *199*

CONTENTS

How from such a chance beginning 200

Ah, how sweet you are, confiding 201

I close her eyes, and keep them tight 201

When in your arms and in our kisses 202

Do not fear, my love; no danger 203

While I seek forbidden pastures 203

Yes, surely, you are my ideal 204

Don't send me off, now that your thirst 205

HORTENSE 205

We stood upon the corner, where 205

DIANE 206

Such magnificent expanse 206

Deep within a lovely garden 207

CLARISSA 208

Do not go into the furious 208

I am helpless. You defeat me 208

Too late your sighs and smiles of promise 209

YOLANDA AND MARIE 210

Both of them know how to honor 210

Which of them shall I fall in love with 210

The bottles are empty, the breakfast was good 211

Youth is leaving me; but daily 212

KATHARINE 212

I spent the day in a heavenly way 212

You lie in my arms so gladly 213

Our platonic souls are surely 214

I love this white and slender body 215

Once I dreamed that I went walking 216

Songless I was, immersed in mourning 218

CONTENTS

KITTY   219
   Her letter leaves me breathless   219
   Swift as a deer, my bark   219
   The joy that kissed me yesterday   220
JENNY   221
   My years now number five-and-thirty   221
IN EXILE   222
   I had, long since, a lovely Fatherland   222

BALLADS

TRAGEDY   224
   "Oh, fly with me and be my love"   224
   The hoar-frost fell on a night in spring   225
   Upon their grave a tree stands now   225
A WOMAN   226
THE ADJURATION   227
ANNO 1829   228
ANNO 1839   229
THE UNKNOWN   231
PSYCHE   233
DAME METTE   233
A MEETING   236
KING HAROLD HARFAGER   238

POEMS FOR THE TIMES

DOCTRINE   240

CONTENTS

A WARNING   *241*

ADAM THE FIRST   *242*

THE TENDENCY   *243*

A PROMISE   *244*

NIGHT THOUGHTS   *245*

THE WEAVERS   *247*

TWO SONGS   *248*

    We laugh and we are troubled   *248*

    It makes a man feel happy   *248*

ROMANCERO AND LATER POEMS

CHARLES I   *250*

THE ASRA   *252*

AMERICA   *253*

A VISIT HOME   *254*

GOOD-FORTUNE AND BAD-LUCK   *257*

TAKE UP THE LYRE   *257*

THE MORNING AFTER   *258*

RETROSPECT   *258*

SOLOMON   *260*

ENFANT PERDU   *261*

THIS VALE OF TEARS   *262*

THE SONG OF SONGS   *263*

SONG OF THE VIVANDIÈRE   *265*

TO MY RELATIONS   *267*

DYING POET   *268*

EPILOG   *269*

THESE LITTLE SONGS   *270*

CONTENTS

DOMESTIC END 271

POTATIONS 272

FINIS 272

IN THE CATHEDRAL 273

FOR "LA MOUCHE" 274

LOTUS-FLOWER 280

IN THE MORNING 281

FOR MATHILDE 282

ANNUAL MOURNING 283

WHERE? 284

IT GOES OUT 285

INDEX OF FIRST LINES 287

AN INTRODUCTION

The centenary of Heinrich Heine's death was celebrated on February 17th, 1956, with a salvo of unreserved appreciations. For the first time in a hundred years, there were no niggling condescensions, no half-hearted excuses for Heine's trenchant but troublesome vulgarities, no sneers at his ambiguous political alignments. There was, on the other hand, plenty of evidence that Heine was being rediscovered as well as reappraised. His poems had always been familiar as pieces of pure lyricism or as lyrics for other men's music—even those who had never opened Heine's pages had heard his poignant syllables intensifying the melodies of Schumann, Schubert, Mendelssohn, Brahms, Franz, Jensen, and Hugo Wolff. But a new emphasis was placed upon the writer who managed to combine magic and common sense, who in the same stanza carefully created and casually destroyed moonlit fantasies and, with a style like a stiletto, cut through universally accepted shams and sanctified stupidities.

It was not only a divided preoccupation with roses and revolution that made Heine so great a paradox; his very being was based on a series of contradictions. A German who dreamed of a greater Germany, he was an expatriate from his homeland and spent most of his life in France. A proudly race-conscious Jew, he became a Protestant and, after a liaison of seven years, married his Catholic mistress. Brought up to be a salesman, he failed in business; although he took his degree as a lawyer, he never engaged in practice. The most dulcet of poets, he was also one of the bitterest and bawdiest; a born romantic, he exposed the spectral hollowness of Romanticism. A cynical wit, he was a political idealist; a journalistic hack, a pot-boiling newspaper correspondent, he was at the same time an impassioned fighter for humanity.

His very name was a compromise. When he was born he was named Harry, after an English business friend of the family; but his childhood companions taunted him with "Haarüh!" (the cry of the local scavenger whipping up his donkey) and the boy began to call himself Heinrich. Later in life the imaginative poet supplied his parents with a glamorous and even patrician background, but their origins were pedestrian. His father, Samson, was the second of eight children born to Chajjim of Bückeburg. Early eighteenth century Jews had no surnames, and when Chajjim moved to Hanover, the Hebrew guttural was smoothed to Heymann, or more Germanically, Heinemann. Eventually the first part of the substitution became the family name, and Chajjim's son settled in Düsseldorf, as Samson Heine. His wife, Betty, was a Van Geldern, and

socially his superior. It was in Düsseldorf that Harry, their
oldest child, was born. Heine claimed that he came into
the world on New Year's Eve, 1800; he liked to say that he
was "one of the first men of the century." The pun was
tempting, and Heine could never resist an epigram. The
registry is no longer in existence, but it is likely that the
year 1800 was given as the year of birth to the authorities
when the boy was eighteen (not, as his parents asserted,
when he was fifteen), so he could escape Prussian military
service in 1815. Documents have come to light which
point to December 13, 1797, as the actual date of his birth.
There were three other children: Charlotte, beloved by
her brother, and two younger brothers, Gustav and Max,
whom the boy distrusted and the grown man rejected.

Samson, a well-liked individual and an incompetent
merchant, hoped that his son would be a successful trades-
man, but Betty had other plans for her first-born. Although
not neglectful of the other children, Heinrich was her
besetting concern. In common with most Jews, she worshipped Napoleon, who had abolished the ghetto; therefore
her son was to be a general in the Napoleonic manner.
"My mother dreamed of me dressed up in golden epau-
lettes," he recalled, "with the most elaborately embroi-
dered uniform at Court." After the fall of the Emperor,
anti-Semitism was restored – in Frankfurt only twenty-
four members of the Mosaic faith were allowed to marry
each year lest the Jewish population increase. Jews were
barred from practically all professions but, since handling
money was regarded as an ignominious business,
were allowed to become money-changers and eventually,

bankers. Accordingly, Betty had a new dream; she saw
Heinrich as another Rothschild. When it became apparent
that the youth was as unfit to mislead investors as to lead
soldiers, Betty had visions of his attaining eminence as one
of the world's great jurists. Nor did these hopes remain
the comforting wish-fulfillments of a doting mother;
Heine was actually prepared for all three dissimilar careers.
That none of them appealed to her son seemed irrevelant
to the determined woman. Fondly but forbiddingly she
frowned on the boy's single talent: his propensity for
making verses. Unhappy to realize that her husband was
a *Luftmensch*, a dreamer who philosophized and quoted
poetry, she would not allow her son to read romances and
she discouraged fairy tales as fanciful nonsense. To her a
poet was a poor devil who turned out rhymes for a few
pennies and always died in the poorhouse.

Although he idolized as well as idealized his mother,
the mature Heine confessed that he inherited nothing
creative from her. J. M. Synge got more aid than any
learning could give him in understanding the folklore of
Ireland from a chink in the floor that let him hear what
the girls in the kitchen were saying. Similarly, Heine
learned the power of simple, idiomatic language and the
richness of folkstuff from an old servant who secretly told
him the forbidden tales and legends.

Heinrich's commonplace, easy-going father failed to share
his wife's grandiose ideas. From the first he had only one

ambition for his son: he wanted him to be a Jew. Accordingly, when Samson became president of "The Society for Performing Humanitarian Acts and Reading the Psalms" and Heinrich was five, the boy was sent to a Hebrew school.

Taught by a typical *melamed*, the boy learned to speak pure Hebrew as well as the German-Yiddish neighborhood jargon; he read verses in the Old Testament, was taught pieces from the Talmud, and recited the ancient prayers. The dietary laws and the various taboos engraved themselves upon his sensitive mind. Impressed with the importance of doing no work on the Sabbath, he refused to help put out a fire one Saturday, saying, "I cannot. I will not. Today is *Shabbes!*"

The two years spent in absorbing Hebraic lore failed to make Heine a practicing Jew, but traces of his training can be found throughout his work. Echoes of the Talmud-Torah school are heard in *Jehuda ben Halevy*, a long glorification of the medieval Hebrew poet, in *Belshazzar*, with its phrasing copied from Hebraic liturgy, in the *Sabbath Song* and the *Hebrew Melodies*. Moreover, Heine's racial inheritance is expressed in the very flavor of his writings, a flavor which is not "bittersweet," as it has often been characterized, but "sweet-sour," the result of generations of cultural as well as culinary pungency.

Heine's lifelong dichotomy began when Betty decided that she had humored her husband enough. She felt that race and religion were all very well in the old days, but these were different times and her son must have a better future than his father. The non-resistant Samson shrugged his shoulders, and Heinrich was taken out of the Jewish *cheder* and placed in a school connected with an old Franciscan monastery. There he encountered the classic tongues, struggled with Latin, and fought a losing battle with Greek. Years later he recalled the crucified Christ that hung in the cloister. It haunted him, he said, with the eyes of a weary pedagog; he remembered how he used to stand before the statue and pray, "O thou poor, eternally tormented God, if everything is possible to Thee, see to it that I do not forget the irregular verbs."

Romance came melodramatically to Heine at sixteen. Josepha or, as he liked to call her, Red Sefchen, was an appropriate first love for a youth who cultivated the Gothic style. She came from a line of executioners and her aunt was considered a witch. When Sefchen tied her long red hair under her chin she looked "as if she had just cut her throat and the blood was running over it in bright red rivulets." Heine gloried as much in his daring as in her wickedness. "Yes," he wrote in his incomplete and high-pitched *Memoirs*, "in spite of the executioner's sword which had beheaded a hundred rogues, and in spite of the infamy which descends on those who have dealings with any of the despised class, I kissed the beautiful daughter of the executioner. I kissed her," he added sententiously, "not only because of my passion for her, but in contempt of society and all the dark prejudices of the social order."

Passion flowered into poetry. Sefchen sang weird ballads and lurid folk-songs to her fascinated admirer, and Heine transmuted them into verses of his own. His earliest poems are the significantly entitled "Dream Pictures," and their very theatricality reflects the mood of bizarre adolescence,

with its macabre fancies and "a grim and gloomy color
like the intimacy which cast its bloody reflection over my
young mind."

Heine was seventeen when his mother relinquished her
dreams of glory and thought of a practical future for her
son. With her eye fixed on her husband's brother, Solomon,
a prominent Hamburg banker, Betty sent Heinrich to a
business school, and a year later, apprenticed him to a
friend in the banking business. When his uncle considered
him ready, the nineteen-year-old lad was brought to
Hamburg. There he immediately fell in love with his
cousin Amalie.

Amalie was sixteen, the self-satisfied, self-centered
daughter of one of Germany's richest men. She flirted
with Heinrich, enjoyed his impetuosity as well as his
adulation, was alternately prim and petulant, and, although
she never pretended to love him, led him to believe that
something might come of his ardor. In this frame of mind,
the hopeful suitor was respectful to her father and grateful
to him when uncle Solomon made him the manager of a
textile shop. Heine was twenty when he saw his name in
gold letters over the store: "Harry Heine and Company."

Instead of being impressed, Amalie sniffed. She was
now eighteen, capricious and calculating. She, too, had a
career to consider. Her nest was already well feathered,
but it was only good housekeeping to provide it with more
and finer feathers. A young poet masquerading as a

merchant was amusing, but a girl must be sensible; it is
only in fairy tales that the princess marries the page.
Besides, the poor relation's poetry was growing a little too
impassioned; it was so intense it was tiresome. "She is
contemptuous of the songs I compose for her," Heine
confided to a friend. He confessed it more sadly in verse.
"I wish that my love-songs were flowers, so she might find
them fair," so runs the first verse of *Ich wollte, meine
Lieder*. "I wish that my love-songs were kisses," says the
second. But, concludes the third, twisting the knife of
sarcasm in the poet's own breast:

> *I wish that these, my love-songs,*
> *Were peas, so firm and fat;*
> *I'd make a nice, rich pea-soup—*
> *And she would relish* THAT!

The twist was not a trick, not merely a mordant anti-
climax; it established itself in the very depths of Heine's
poetry. It was the false shrug that concealed the real pain.
In a typically youthful mixture of anguish and self-pity,
he wrote in his *Letters*, "To be absent from her—to bear
passion consuming one's vitals—that is the torture of the
damned. But to be near her, and to pine during an eternity
of weeks for the greatest of blessings, a single look from her,
that is enough to force blasphemies from the most pious
soul." . . . "She loves me not – but you must murmur
the 'not' very softly. The words 'She loves' include Paradise and the life immortal. The little negative contains all
of Hell, which is no less eternal."

Amalie, it happened, fancied herself in love—but not
with Heine. Instead of concentrating on his customers,
Heine was imagining himself a knightly hero, rescuing
his beloved from the sordid life of the city, carrying her on
wings of song to the exotic Ganges, while Amalie was
about to be betrothed to a "well connected" friend of her
father's. The end was foreseen by everyone except Heine.
He quarreled continually with his uncle, whom he both
admired and belittled— "My mother read fine literature,
and so I became a poet. My uncle's mother read tales of
robbers, so *her* son became a banker." Less than a year
after its debut, the firm of Harry Heine went into bank-
ruptcy, whereupon Solomon, a kind of tolerant tyrant,
sent his impractical nephew to Bonn to study law. Amalie,
yielding to sentiment and a feeling of relief, bade Heine
an affectionate farewell, and implied that she would wait
for him. Two years later she made a proper marriage with
her father's friend, Johann Friedländer, a Prussian land-
owner.

One might have predicted that Amalie's flightiness
would hurt the young poet's pride, but Heine acted as if
nature itself had betrayed him. He never recovered from
the blow. It dominated his thought; his poetry seethes
with a sense of wrong. Not once, but a hundred times he
retold the story of the faithless girl who turned from her
poor but true love to a comfortable, middle-class marriage.
What was youthful incompatibility turned into an
elemental treachery. Years later, when Heine was a
cynical roué, he met a young girl who reminded him of
Amalie, and in a poem to *Jenny* he again gave vent to the

anguish of "the old dream that will not die." In one of
the key poems in the *Lyrical Intermezzo* he attempts to
forestall the charge that his misery is self-induced.
Vergiftet sind meine Lieder, he cries not only to Amalie
but to the world:

> *My songs, you say, are poisoned,*
> *How else, love, could it be?*
> *You have, with deadly magic,*
> *Poured poison into me.*
>
> *My songs, you say, are poisoned,*
> *And well I know it, too.*
> *I carry a thousand serpents*
> *And, love, among them—you.*

Amalie was not only his blonde angel but his dark
demon. Eve had become the serpent, and Paradise was a
dream of fools in hell.

Heine's university life was a tragi-comedy. At Bonn,
thanks to August Wilhelm von Schlegel, he learned
literature rather than law. Schlegel, older brother of the
philosopher, Karl Wilhelm Friederich, was Germany's
greatest translator of Shakespeare and an authority on
the English poets. Caught up in a new luxuriance of sound,
Heine spouted Shakespearean purple passages and the lyrics
of Byron, with whom he quickly identified himself. Never-

theless, Heine realized that if he was to be a lawyer, he would have to devote less time to poetics and more time to torts, contracts, the code, and the Common Law. Göttingen was the place for this, and there at twenty-two Heine subjected himself to the discipline of a strict curriculum. He hated every dull moment of it. "If I had not been intimidated by the distance, I would have gone straight back to Bonn." Boredom turned into bitterness when the rumor about Amalie's marital status became a fact. He drank, and suffered from stomach trouble. He brawled with other students, and got into difficulties with the authorities. He revenged himself upon Amalie by consorting with prostitutes, and contracted the disease which crippled him in his forties and killed him in his fifties. What was diagnosed as a "consumption of the spinal marrow" – an ailment treated by cautery with hot steel and application of leeches – is now known to be syphilis.

At twenty-three, the symptoms which any diagnostician today would recognize – the dragging foot, the semi-paralysis, the increasing blindness – had not manifested themselves. Heine's nervous hypersensitivity, however, was apparent in the pale brow, the hollow temples, the thin cheeks, and delicate hands never at rest. The mouth did not yet wear the sneer of the middle-age cynic nor the sad fixity of the doomed invalid, but its sensuous contour was already deepened by a satiric twitch. The warmth of the full lips was contradicted by the cold blue eyes, clear and appraising, denying the mockery of the mouth. It was his mocking spirit, culminating in a threatened duel, which was responsible for Heine's six months' suspension from

Göttingen. In a confusion of nostalgia and masochism, he
went to Hamburg,"lovely cradle of his sorrows,"and tortured himself. Pain was concentrated in poetry, and poems
were the distillation of his pain: *Aus meinen grossen
Schmerzen mach ich die kleinen Lieder*. In his twenty-fourth
year he made another determined effort to complete his law
courses, and forced himself to attend the University of Berlin.

He remained in Berlin two years and two months, long
enough to get acquainted with Leopold Zunz, who was
to become one of the great Jewish scholars; Christian
Dietrich Grabbe, the so-called "drunken Shakespeare,"
who wrote the violently amoral *Theodor von Gothland*
in his twenty-first year; Rahel Varnhagen, at whose salon
he met the leading literati; and Georg Wilhelm Friedrich
Hegel, the iconoclastic philosopher who inspired Marx.
It was Hegel's coldly brilliant rationalism that fascinated
the young student. A flashing passage in Heine's *Memoirs*
reveals the curious kinship between teacher and pupil:
"One night, when we were standing at a window, I spoke
rhapsodically about the stars as 'the abodes of the blest.'
Whereupon the master grumbled, 'The stars? A light
eruption on the face of the sky.' 'But,' I persisted, 'is there
no place where virtue is rewarded?'— 'So,' he retorted,
'you demand a tip for being good to your mother and not
poisoning your brothers!' "

Hegel's influence did not manifest itself until much
later in Heine's life; only an occasional trace of it appears
in his first volume, published a few weeks after his twenty-
fifth birthday. *Gedichte* (*Poems*) is characterized by its
subtitle, *Junge Leiden* (*Youthful Sorrows*) and especially

its opening section, *Traumbilder* (*Dream Pictures*). The
half-fantastic, half-funereal mood is extended in the
narratives which include *Poor Peter*, *The Prisoner's Song*,
The Message, and, in nostalgic measures set to Schumann's
ringing music, *The Grenadiers*. In the group entitled
Lieder (*Songs*) there is heard a new poetic speech, a
common, almost conversational idiom which grew into the
purest expression of German lyrical poetry. The autobiographical disclosures, soon to be apparent to the most
casual reader, are disguised; but the struggle between the
yearning romanticist and the disillusioned dreamer are
only half-concealed.

The hard light of reason breaks through a mist of magic
in *Dialog on Paderborn Heath* and *Absolutely!* But the
singing transcends the cynicism, and Heine caught the
simple rhythms and spontaneous speech of ordinary people
so skillfully that one of the critics praised *The Grenadiers*
as a moving translation of a French folk-song.

At twenty-six, Heine returned to the University of
Göttingen, his fourth attempt to complete a college career.
"I have devoted myself to jurisprudence," he wrote to
Moses Moser, a business man whom Heine admired
because he not only had a passionate pity for mankind but
tried to do something to alleviate its ills. "I read records
and drink beer. I am also being ruined by love, though
not the one-sided love for a particular individual that
devastated me in the past. I am no longer single-hearted
in my devotion. Just as I insist on a double portion of
beer, so now I must have a double portion of love. I am
in love—desperately—with the Venus of Medici at the

Library and the pretty cook at Bauer's. Neither of my
passions is reciprocated." The tone was light, for Heine
wanted to believe he had freed himself from the distress
of his one-sided "love" by sublimating it in long lyrical
sequences. But he was self-deceived.

The autobiographical poems were preceded by two
violent but ineffective plays. *Schicksalsdramen* (fate-driven
dramas) were all the rage in Heine's twenties; in *Almansor*
and *William Ratcliff* Heine, fancying himself Marlowe
if not Shakespeare, ran the gamut of rhetoric, flung
soliloquies about, and alternated violent declamations with
discourses on the comfort of faith and the power of moonlight. He also began a prose work, *The Rabbi of Bacharach*,
which he conceived of as "an ever-burning lamp in the
cathedral of God," but which was never completed.

In 1823 Heine published the two dramas with a *Lyrical
Intermezzo*. The lurid tragedies were promptly forgotten,
but those who read the straightforward verses in the
Lyrical Intermezzo knew they would never forget them.
For one thing, the language was an unbelievable combin-
ation of simplicity and subtlety. Using the vocabulary of
the people, Heine achieved a heart-breaking poignance;
condensing turbulent emotions into tight little quatrains,
he fashioned stanzas that were both epigrammatic and
eloquent. The utmost refinements of language were
sharpened by purposeful dissonances of vulgarity. It is no
wonder that dozens of the poems are thought of as folk-
songs; they seem to be relics of oral rather than written
literature. One cannot trace their origin in textbooks;
they are written miracles of organization constructed with

such deceptive artlessness that they appear casual to the point of carelessness.

The personal element in the poetry is as pronounced as the technique. As though to underline the autobiographical import of his work, Heine prefaced later editions of the *Lyrical Intermezzo* with a quatrain which told the reader explicitly that the poet had poured all his hopes, fears, and frustrations into the poems. His heart beat on every page. The story is trite enough: the shyness and wonder of first love, short-lived ecstasy and nervous apprehension, sudden betrayal, bitterness, and final despair. The poems begin with light and happy colors; the mood is that of a May morning; little breezes blow through the scented lime-trees. The end is dark and tortured; autumn winds rattle dry branches, stars fall from the sky; the mood is midnight's drear premonition of death. The image of Amalie is everywhere. It blurs and changes into a lotus-flower, a languishing palm tree, a king's daughter, while Heine becomes the passion-inspiring moon, the lordly pine, the princely lover, and Hamburg is transmogrified into a hell of memories as well as a heavenly haven which the poet can never hope to attain.

It was at the wedding of his sister, Charlotte, that he noticed Therese. Therese, Amalie's younger sister, was an awkward twelve-year-old when Heine had left Berlin four years ago. Now, at sixteen, she was a shy but attractive girl whose likeness to his lost love startled Heine.

He fell in love with the troublesome resemblance, hoping for a possible union with Solomon's young daughter and fearing the renewal of another unhappy infatuation with one who was barely aware of him. He struggled with what was becoming an obsession. "He who loves for the first time, even vainly, is a god," he wrote in one of his revealing verses. "But he who loves for the second time, still unrequited, is a fool."

The result of the double attachment is *Die Heimkehr* (*The Home-coming*), a continuation and expansion of the *Lyrical Intermezzo*. The background is Hamburg —"my Tartarus and my Elysium"— and the home-coming is a bitter repetition of Heine's old sorrow. There are moments of relief as the scene shifts to the seashore and the poet tries to forget his unhappiness in the salt spray, the shouting winds, and an occasional love-affair. But most of it takes place in the city he loved and loathed, where, pathetically recorded in the most polished verse, he paces the streets, yearning for his beloved, and sees his Doppelgänger, his phantom double, wringing his hands in the cold moonlight. The famous *Ich weiss nicht was soll es bedeuten*, which should have been placed among the ballads and narratives, is put near the beginning, the second poem in the sequence, for Heine wants to tell the readers it is not only a legend but a personal experience. The Loreley is Amalie, cool, blonde, golden in every sense. She, too, is a fatal lure, an apparition adorning herself on the heights; while the poor lover, blind to the reefs of reality, is dashed to destruction.

Heine would have been the first to appreciate the irony

that, less than a century after they had been written,
many of his poems had become his country's favorite
folk-songs. Even Hitler, who burned all Heine's poetry, had
to preserve *The Loreley*. He did it in typically Hitlerian
fashion. Unable to expunge the cherished verses from the
song-books, he credited the music to Ferdinand Silcher,
who had given the poem a sentimental tune, and ordered
that the words should be followed by the designation:
"Author Unknown."

The law degree was still to be attained, and Heine was
self-conscious about being a student at the age of twenty-
six. But first there was a tramping expedition, a trip which
formed the basis for *Die Harzreise* (*The Harz Journey*)
and which included a call on Goethe. The Goethe meeting
was not so much a visit as a visitation. For once Heine,
usually so loquacious, was tongue-tied. All the carefully
rehearsed speeches vanished; he seemed a presumptuous
mortal who had forced himself upon the chief Olympian
deity. When asked what travel experience had impressed
him most, Heine mumbled,"The plums between Jena
and Weimar were very sweet." ("All through the long
winter nights I had thought over the deep ideas and
elevated sentiments I would exchange with Goethe if I
should ever meet him. And when finally I saw him, I told
him that the Saxon plums tasted good.") Goethe smiled
coolly; but he froze when, in answer to a query about
writing, Heine said he was working on a Faust. "A—
Faust!" flashed the Jupiter of Weimar, and Heine fancied
he heard thunder in the room. "And have you any other
business in Weimar?" inquired Goethe icily. Heine gulped.

"When I leave your Excellency, my business in Weimar is ended." The Harz journey was over.

Back in Göttingen Heine prepared to take the long-deferred degree. He was in his twenty-eighth year when he underwent examination as candidate for Doctor of Law. First, however, he had to do something which deepened the division in his already split nature: he had to stop calling himself a Jew and present himself to the Faculty as a Christian. It was common practice and, since the legal profession was not open to Jews, the step was taken for granted. "No one in my family opposes the step," commented Heine. "No one except me." He repeated the remark with grim variations. "I shall be sorry if you find anything to say in favor of my baptism," he wrote to Moser. "If I could have made a living by stealing spoons without going to prison, I would never have allowed the christening." Nevertheless, he was baptized, and with a new, unquestionably Teutonic name: Christian Johann Heinrich Heine. In less than a year he regretted the sham conversion from whch he had gained nothing. On the contrary, he suffered from the change. He had lost caste, hope of advancement, and self-respect; he was, he said, "despised alike by Jews and Gentiles."

Humor saved him, even though it was the humor of self-inflicted irony. He had done the right thing by his family, and no one could expect him to be a devout, church-going Christian. "No Jew," he said, "can ever believe in the divinity of any other Jew." Meanwhile, he became a Doctor of Law and a Protestant. He was an attorney; he had kept his promise. Two days after re-

ceiving his degree, he went to Hamburg, where, welcomed
by his uncle Solomon, he went to temple. "I have become
a typical Christian," he wrote Moser. "I sponge on the rich
Jews." On another occasion, he wrote, "I had Shabbes
dinner with Cohen who heaped fiery *Kugel* on my head,
and penitently I ate the sacred national dish, which has
done more to preserve Judaism than all the numbers of
Cohen's *Journal*. Of course it has enjoyed a much wider
circulation."

It was at this time that Heine's intermittent headaches
began to be constant. No one thought of them as warnings
of a dread disease—some of his friends insisted that Heine
was cultivating the proverbial poetic temperament—but
after Heine's late twenties he was always physically racked.
In an effort to alleviate the pain, and with Solomon's
blessing, he went to the seaside at Norderney. For the
time being, the ocean acted as a great restorative. The
element excited him with its ever-changing surface and
secret depths. He wove fantasies about all-too-human gods
and complaisant sea-nymphs; he visited with fishermen
and flirted with their daughters; he thought of the myth
of the Flying Dutchman, a kind of acquatic Wandering
Jew, and added variations which had not existed until
Heine invented them, and which Wagner, with characteristic Wagnerian nonchalance, stole from Heine. Everything at Norderney was new material for the convalescent.
Some of it was expressed in whimsical prose; most of it
was channeled into the tumbling rhythms of *Die Nordsee*
(*The North Sea*), a series of polyrhythmical poems, a new
experiment, anticipating the free verse orgies by a century.

The biographer-analyst will find significance in Heine's choice of a symbol. Shelley's bird, indicative of his soaring spirit, is the skylark; Keats is identified with the nightingale; Poe and his raven are inseparable; but Heine saw himself riding desperate waves with the restless wanderer, the wind-driven and homeless sea-gull.

Heine never opened an office; it is unlikely that he ever seriously contemplated the practice of law. Instead he became what he always planned to be: a professional poet. His early poems had elicited many pleasant though not superlative comments; his satiricial collections of *Reisebilder* (*Travel Pictures*), written *con brio*, were praised for their boldness as well as their brilliance; the poetry assembled cumulatively in *Buch der Lieder* (*Book of Songs*) was an unorthodox success. Critics were bewildered by his blend of sentiment and mockery, his unique technique of antithesis which he called his "malicious-lyrical two-strophe manner," his kaleidoscopic shifting of ideas, and his cavalier use of German idioms. His predecessors had always treated the German language as though it were a stern and stolid matron—half-goddess, half-schoolmistress—with whom one took no liberties. Heine wrote as though she were a light-of-love who had chosen him as companion for a madcap holiday. Professors grumbled, reviewers equivocated, but readers were delighted. Heine was happy; he had achieved not only a career but a following.

He loafed and luxuriated in travel. He sojourned in England four months, remained some time in Munich, and spent a creative half-year in Italy. New ideas assailed him,

new political upheavals matured him. "Every age has its
task," he wrote. "And what is the great task of our day?
It is this: emancipation . . . Freedom is a new religion, the
religion of our age."

The thought of freedom smoldered in the breast of the
rebellious poet; it sprang into flame when he heard that
the citizens of Paris had risen and had dethroned the
tyrant, Charles X. The great day had dawned, the people
had won, and Heine proclaimed himself the son of the
Revolution. He fully expected the fire to spread, but
Germany was quick to stamp out the sparks before they
blazed through Europe. A planned *Judenkrawall*, a vicious
anti-Jewish pogrom, raged through Hamburg. Shops
were looted, the synagogues were stoned, Heine's volumes
were among the Jewish books thrown on the bonfires.
Heine was heartsick, yet he still hoped that a new regime
might be ushered in without bloodshed. "It depends upon
the freedom of the press whether the word 'revolution'
will be uttered in quiet discussion by orderly assemblies,
or in rage by uncontrollable mobs." The press, however,
was anything but free; Heine's publisher was threatened
by the censor, and his attorney told the poet that the irons
attached to political prisoners were particularly cold and
heavy.

In 1831, on May 1, a significant day for a rebel in the
"magic month of May"—Heine crossed the Rhine. In his
thirty-fourth year he was on his way to liberty and,
although he did not know it, exile. All that he knew was
that he was breathing the heady air of Paris. "The crowds
astonished me—the people were so gay; they looked as

though they had stepped from the plates of a fashion
magazine . . . The men are courteous and the women
amiable. If a man, jostling me, did not excuse himself,
I could be sure he was one of my own countrymen; if a
woman failed to smile back at me, I knew she had either
eaten sauerkraut or read Klopstock in the original . . . It is
true that, on street corners here and there, the words
Liberté, Egalité, Fraternité had been rubbed off. But,"
Heine concluded drily, "a honeymoon cannot last forever."

While it lasted, Heine relished the honeymoon. To be
exact, he indulged in a series of honeymoons before he
settled down to work and a kind of disorderly domesticity.
He roamed about without supervision and wrote without
censorship. He was equally charmed by the paintings in
the Louvre, the performances at the Opera, the horrors
of the Morgue, and the girls of Montmartre. He wrote to
the composer, Ferdinand Hiller: "If anyone asks you how
I am enjoying myself, say, 'Like a fish in sea.' Better
still, say that when one fish asks another how he is
enjoying himself, the fish replies, 'Like Heine in Paris.' "

Paris was not only his Parnassus but his Venusberg.
Heine may have been more promiscuous than
Tannhäuser, but he was also a more accurate reporter.
Besides *The Song of Songs*, which opens so reverently
and ends so raucously, the amatory portraits in
Verschiedene (*A Garland of Girls*) are graphic and
sharply differentiated. *Seraphine*, with its echoes of the
sea, is unashamedly sentimental; *Angelique* is bantering
and disillusioned; *Hortense* is teasing, tender without
being mawkish; *Clarissa* is a distorted memory of Amalie;

Katharine is both serious and sensual; *Yolanda and Marie*
is ironically lewd; *Diane* is frankly ribald. One believes in
the actuality of these women, in their flesh-and-blood dif-
ferences, where we can never believe in Herrick's Julia or
Anthea or Electra or Corinna or his other imaginary
mistresses, none of whom can be distinguished from the
others. Like Herrick, Heine was plain-spoken; he, too,
employed simple stanza structures and a straightforward
idiom. Unlike Herrick, Heine took no pains to smooth
away either the logically rough contours of his verse or
refine the naturalistic coarseness of his subject matter.

Théophile Gautier drew a vivid picture of Heine at
thirty-five, about a year after he took up residence in
Paris. Aware of Heine's later decline, Gautier remembered him as "a German Apollo – his forehead high
and white, pure as marble. His blue eyes burned with
inspiration; his cheeks were gracefully rounded, not
romantically pale as was then the fashion. A slight
embonpoint, to give way to a truly Christian emaciation,
rounded the lines of his body." Besides Gautier, Heine
met the ageing but still vigorous Lafayette, as well as
such celebrities as Hugo, who sponsored him, George
Sand, who mothered him, Dumas, Balzac, Alfred de
Musset, and Gérard de Nerval, all of whom accepted him
immediately in spite of his strangeness and his accent
which, according to Sainte-Beuve, was "very Germanic
and very disagreeable."

Inevitably Heine became embroiled in politics. He
renewed an old friendship with Ludwig Börne, who, like
Heine, was an expatriate German Jew; then, because

Börne leaned too far to the dangerous Left, shamelessly repudiated him. An uncompromising insurgent, Heine learned to compromise, compelled (he insisted) to earn a living by his wits if not by his convictions. He became a foreign correspondent and was immensely flattered when the powerful Thiers declared that Heine wrote the best French in Paris. To bring about better relations between France and Germany he accepted a French government subsidy of 4,800 francs a year—something which, later, was held against him as a suspiciously venal if not treacherous act. He aligned himself with the Centrists, supported the bourgeoisie, and was, for a while, an unscrupulous journalist. The symptoms of his disease manifested themselves noticeably, but Heine appeared nonchalant. "I am one of pot-bellied Louis Philippe's camp-followers; my cheeks are tanned; I wear bright coats and gay vests; two fingers of my right hand are crippled."

Feeling that he had betrayed himself by selling out to the enemy, he announced that he was quitting politics and devoting himself to art, religion, and philosophy. Converted to Saint-Simonism, a combined forerunner of Christian Socialism and Christian Science, he was an ardent disciple for a year, then grew disillusioned when the "physico-political" religion was unable to cope with the corrupt excesses of the day. He escaped a cholera epidemic, but his headaches developed a new malevolence. Börne pictured Heine at thirty-five lamentably frayed, "worn out, like an old shirt. I watched him going down the street looking like a withered leaf."

Heine was thirty-seven when he met Crescentia Eugénie
Mirat in her aunt's shabby glove shop. She was not yet
nineteen, an illegitimate child born in the provinces.
She was Heine's complete opposite—Catholic, lazy, devoid
of humor, untidy, and ignorant—she could neither read
nor write. It was her young earthiness that attracted
Heine and, though she proved to be an incompetent
housekeeper and a hopeless cook, she held him. Besides,
she was bold; she met the accomplished libertine more
than half-way. Although she had no objection to casual
assignations, Heine wanted constant companionship, and
the couple decided to live together. The aunt shrugged
her shoulders and bargained a bit; the price, according to
the niece, was set at three thousand francs.

Heine hated the pretentious name—Crescentia, he
said, stuck in his throat—so he called her Mathilde. He
tried to educate her but, after years of instruction, she
read with difficulty and the letters she wrote were misspelt
scrawls. That her lover may have been an important
writer never occurred to her. When someone informed
her that Heine was a great poet, she laughed. "Oh, but
you're wrong. If my Henri were a great poet he would
certainly have told me." It was a curious menage: the
wittiest man in Europe and the stupidest child. She
disliked cooking, so whenever Heine was in a good mood,
she wheedled him out of the house and into a restaurant.
Heine detested mutton, so when she did cook, they had

mutton. Pauline, a woman of even less virtue than
Mathilde, was her best friend, and drove Heine frantic
with her strident chatter. A still greater curse was Cocotte,
Mathilde's pet parrot. Heine would swear at Cocotte in
exasperated German, and the bird would scream back in
high-pitched French, "We are both wildly happy living
here together," he confided to his friend Lewald. "That
is, I never have a peaceful moment day or night."

Nevertheless, the liaison lasted. There were countless
quarrels, spasms of jealousy, threats of departure, but the
bonds held tight. Mathilde knew that Heine was unfaithful
to her, even with her friends; but she also knew that a
passing amour flattered his vanity and, as far as she was
concerned, the sexual act meant little. Heine's jealousy,
on the other hand, was deeper. For one thing, he was nineteen years older, and his past had made him abnormally
fearful. Having lost so much, the thought of another loss
drove him into frenzies. Mathilde grew older, complacent
and corpulent, but he never ceased to be sentimental
about her. The threat of a duel (brought about by Heine's
libellous innuendoes concerning Börne and Frau Wohl,
a respectably married woman) made him realize that,
should he be killed, Mathilde would be left without legal
rights. So, seven years after setting up the first of many
domiciles with his mistress, Heine married her. The duel
never happened, and Heine wrote to his friend, Alexandre
Weill, "That terrible Frau Wohl has had her revenge.
But I will have mine. Returning from the church I made
a Will, leaving everything to my wife. I left it to her,
however, on one condition – that she marry immediately

after my death. In that way, I will be sure that at least one man is sorry I am no longer living."

In his forties Heine was plagued with double suffering: a longing for his native soil, a yearning which sometimes became unbearable, and the slow but relentless progress of his disease. His head throbbed incessantly; a creeping paralysis affected his arm; his left foot was so lame that children cruelly imitated his limp. In spite of this, he looked deceptively healthy—he complained about his unpoetic weight—and he busied himself with a wide variety of projects from a running commentary on a set of engravings, *Shakespeare's Girls and Women*, with particularly trenchant considerations of Cressida, Cordelia, and Jessica, to the gay prose of *Memoirs of von Schnabelewopski*, a romping divertissement which mingles satire, fantasy, social criticism, coarse lampoons, burlesque autobiography, and a kind of caustic nonsense. He begins an account of a bad dinner by saying, "For the first course we had no soup," remarks that the women of Hamburg are more interested in pastries than in passion because Cupid's arrows "instead of hitting their hearts lodged in their stomachs," and apologizes to the reader for a passage about prostitutes: "If I dragged you down into low company, it may comfort you to know that the descent cost you less than it did me."

The poetry of this period is as mocking as the prose. *Atta Troll* is a phantasmagoria of symbolic figures and obscure dialectics, interesting today only to the student of literature; Heine called it "a mad Midsummer Night's Dream" and "the last wild woodnote of romanticism."

Germany: *A Fairy Tale*, a more orderly sequel to *Atta Troll*, is a political satire, full of rough rhymes and rougher humor. A single poem written about this time ("A Visit Home"), which graphically pictures Heine's meeting with his mother in Germany after an absence of thirteen years, is strangely effective as well as affecting in its fusion of nostalgia, outspoken longing, and evasiveness.

There were other things to keep Heine busy and distract him from preoccupation with Mathilde and his illness. At forty-seven he became a contributor to *Vorwärts*, a progressive weekly, one of whose editors was Karl Marx. It was under Marx's influence that Heine wrote the angry *Zeitgedichte* (*Poems for the Times*), most of which appeared in the journal. They burn with the fire of a young insurgent and the indignation of a mature and challenging lover of liberty, outraged at the dictatorial State and the loss of individual rights. *Neue Gedichte* (*New Poems*) incorporated the timely verses and added many others in the vein which Heine had popularized and whose deceptively flat utterance was imitated by the Spanish Gustavo Adolfo Bécquer and the English A. E. Housman, both of whom wrote of lost love and desperate disenchantment in clipped measures and a severely restricted vocabulary. Heine's two selves, the political liberal and the public libertine, joined in blazing protests and exhibits of sexual bravado, and once again the poet was in trouble. The long arm of the Prussian censor stretched across national boundaries and extended to Paris. Heine was blacklisted and threatened with a prison sentence. Although he escaped being jailed, his finances were depleted and his security shattered.

He was now fifty years old. Mathilde grew shrewish and the illness grew steadily worse. Even at this stage Heine might have been saved had the doctors been less ignorant; but, although the pale spirochete had been isolated, physicians during the middle of the nineteenth century were only experimenting with mercury and iodine. Heine was bled, cauterized, poulticed, and bled again in the hope that the "bad" blood would drain away. "I kiss," he wrote to Ferdinand Lassalle, "but I feel nothing. Part of my tongue is paralyzed; everything I eat tastes like earth. My speech-organs are so crippled I can barely articulate; my frame has shrunk...I know I cannot be saved, but I expect to hang on another miserable two or three years. Between you and me, death is the least thing to fear—it is the dying which is so terrible."

Heine was mistaken about the time still allotted to him. He was a long time dying—ten more miserable years, most of them twisted in agony—as he lay helpless and hopeless. But he was Heine to the last. As the pains penetrated every nerve, the witticisms sharpened and the satire stabbed deeper. The reader, however, could not suspect the torture in such sidelong thrusts as:

Music at a wedding always reminds me of military music played just before a battle.

I will not say that women have no character; rather, they have a new one every day.

AN INTRODUCTION

Offered the choice between a bad conscience and a tooth-ache, I would always choose the former—it hurts less.

We praise the poet, the preacher, and the actor who move us to tears—a talent which they share with the common onion.

The aristocracy are asses—asses who talk about horses.

(Of Léon Halévy, brother of the musician who wrote "La Juive") He is as dull as if his brother had composed him.

(Of Alfred de Musset) Everyone has some weakness, and Musset is vain. Vanity is one of his four heels of Achilles.

(Of the pedantic Professor Saalfeld) It is significant that Napoleon's detractors all ended horribly. Castlereagh cut his throat; Louis the Eighteenth rotted to death on his throne; and Professor Saalfeld still teaches at Göttingen.

(Of a woman who boasted of her Grecian beauty) Truly she is like the Venus de Milo in many ways. She is unbelievably old; she has no teeth; and her body is covered with yellow spots.

My constitution is even worse than the Constitution of Prussia.

*All I ask is a simple cottage, a decent bed, good food,
some flowers in front of my window, and a few trees
beside my door. Then, if the Lord wanted to make me
completely happy he would do one thing more for me.
He would grant me the pleasure of seeing six or seven of
my enemies dangling from those trees. With a heart
moved by compassion, I would forgive them all the
wrongs they have done me, for we must learn to forgive
our enemies. But not until they are hanged.*

*Women have just one way of making us happy, but
thirty thousand different ways of making us miserable.*

Heine's will to live kept him through a decade of dying.
He took to his "mattress grave" when he was in his early
fifties; it was, he says, "a tomb without quiet, a death
without the privileges of the dead. Dead men do not have
to spend money, write letters, or make books." He joked
about everything except "my sickness and my work—and
the first scarcely leaves me an hour for the second."
Impotent, unable to lift a pen, he still felt involved in the
human struggle. "To me poetry has always been an
instrument, a sort of divine plaything. If you would honor
me, lay a sword rather than a wreath upon my coffin; for
I was, first of all, a soldier in the wars for the liberation
of mankind."

For six years Heine lay in a funereal gloom; the room
was kept in semi-darkness because light hurt the sufferer's

eyes. His figure had shrunk; his face, a gray alabaster, was hardly distinguishable from the pillow. His eye-sockets were dark pits; one eye was completely closed and the other focussed with difficulty. Few visitors climbed the narrow staircase and, in order to recognize them, Heine had to lift a palsied eyelid with his hand to make sure who was calling. Bed-sores and griping spasms kept him from lying long in one position, and he had to be shifted constantly. Mathilde bounced in and out like a sympathetic child, a cheerful child with no inhibitions. Although she was no longer young or pretty, Heine was still jealous of every man in Paris. "But what can I do!" he moaned. "How can a sick and helpless man compete with half a million rivals—all of them healthy!" As his illness dragged on, there were less and less visitors. The embassy no longer knew where he lodged; the Paris directory ceased to list his name. After Berlioz had come to see him, Heine remarked, "Berlioz always was original!"

Suddenly, at fifty-four, he announced his return to God. His religious need, he said, did not crave the peal of bells or glitter of altar candles, but he was anxious to be at peace with God and the world. "Lying on one's deathbed —hearing nothing but hammering, scolding, the rattle of carriages and the pounding of someone practicing the piano—one becomes sentimental . . . Since I myself am in need of God's grace, I have granted all my enemies an amnesty. Poems which have belittled the goodness of God have been consigned to the flames. It is better that the verses should burn rather than the versifier." Nevertheless, the return to faith was not without its Heinesque twist.

He told Alfred Meissner that if he could support himself
on crutches he would go straight to a church, and when
Meissner expressed surprise, Heine went on, "Where else
should I go on crutches? If I could get along without
crutches I would stroll along the bright boulevards or
kick up my heels in the Bal Mabille."

In the third year of his dying, Heine came to life again.
He astonished the doctors by sitting up and reading with
little strain, dictating, and sometimes even writing. There
were new and incredibly vigorous poems: *Hebrew
Melodies*, full of memories and characteristic discords,
gruesome *Narratives*, powerful *Lamentations*, and lyrics
as image-crowded and idiosyncratic as anything he ever
wrote. Collected and published in *Romancero*, they were
so well liked that four editions were printed within two
months, and when *Les oeuvres complètes de Henri Heine*
brought him an admiring new audience, Heine enjoyed
the success more than anything he could imagine except
a return of his vitality.

Stimulated by the plaudits, Heine planned a two-part
work of prose and poetry, began a set of *Confessions*, and
amplified his *Memoirs*. His condition was degenerating
rapidly; at fifty-eight he was near the end. He had
employed secretaries from time to time, but in his last
year, there came into his life a woman who served as
amanuensis, companion, and inamorata. Mathilde opposed
her, but she took possession and kept Heine alive with
love and poetry for eight more months. A literary
adventuress who went by many names, at this time she
was Elise Krienitz; later she wrote under the pseudonym

of Camille Selden and, as the mistress of Taine, was also
known as Mme. Von Belgern. To Heine, who fell in love
with her, she was his passion-flower, his lotus-blossom,
his lovely angel of death. Chiefly, however, he called
her "La Mouche," partly because the seal she wore was
engraved with a fly, partly because she flitted so lightly
about. "It makes me happy that I shall soon put a chaste
kiss upon your sweet face," he wrote, although he could
scarcely see the letters. "The words would suggest something less platonic were I a man but, alas, I am little more
than a spirit. This may please you, but it does not please
me at all!" Never was he so devotedly in love, and never
was he so incapable of consummating his desire. The
knowledge of his inability made him more miserable
than all his pains. He was Tantalus and Prometheus in
one: a continually tempted, frustrated Tantalus and a
despairing Prometheus chained to his impotence.

Poem after poem, palpitating with dreams of the
unattainable, poured from the dying man. *For "La
Mouche,"* Heine's swan-song, is a love poem, an essay in
philosophy, and a tragic valedictory. In it the poet
summarizes his present inner conflict and his past
self-division, his mixed inheritance and his attempt to
unite the "blithe Hellene" with the "God-yearning Jew."
Only once or twice had Heine put so much of himself in
so few pages.

There was no time for more. Only two things sustained
him: drugs and his almost pathological attachment to
"La Mouche." The February of 1856 was unusually
bitter, and Heine's cold body was torn with cramps which

even laudanum could not quiet. For days he lay conscious of every agonizing twinge. Nevertheless, the wit continued to flicker. When asked whether he wanted a priest to shrive him, Heine grimaced, *"Dieu me pardonnera, c'est son métier"*—"God will pardon me; that's his business."

The end came at four o'clock on the morning of February 17th. Ironically, the only woman with him was neither "La Mouche" nor Mathilde but an emergency nurse. She heard him coughing. "Paper!" he gasped. "Paper! Pencil!" Those were his last words. No man ever died more in character.

Louis Untermeyer

POEMS OF

HEINRICH HEINE

YOUTHFUL SORROWS

∿∿∿∿∿∿∿∿∿∿∿∿∿∿∿

PREFACE TO THE
"BOOK OF SONGS"

Das ist der alte Märchenwald

It was the old, enchanted wood;
    The linden was in flower.
The cold, white magic of the moon
    Inflamed me with its power....

I wandered on, and as I went
    I heard the heavens ringing;
Of love and the keen ache of love
    The nightingale was singing.

Of love and the keen ache of love
    She sang; of tears and laughter –
So sad her mirth, so sweet her sobs,
    That dead dreams followed after.

3

YOUTHFUL SORROWS

I wandered on, and as I went
    A wide space lay before me.
And there, with towering spires, there rose
    A castle huge and stormy.

Barred were its windows; over all
    Lay grief and silence, giving
The sense that in these wasted walls
    Nothing but Death was living.

Before the door there lay a Sphinx,
    Half-horrible, half-human;
A lion's form in body and claws,
    The forehead and breast a woman.

A woman fair! Her marble gaze
    Was sensuous and commanding.
Her mute lips curved into a smile
    Of secret understanding.

The nightingale so sweetly sang,
    What use was my resistance –
I kissed her radiant face, and that
    Altered my whole existence.

For lo, the marble statue woke;
    The stone was touched with fire;
She drank the fervor of my kiss
    With an unslaked desire.

YOUTHFUL SORROWS

She drank my very breath from me
    And then, with lustful ardor,
Her lion's claws sank in my flesh,
    Holding me closer, harder.

O exquisite torture, rapturous wounds!
    O pain and pleasure unending!
For while I drank the kiss of her mouth
    The claws were tearing and rending.

The nightingale sang, "O wondrous Sphinx,
    O Love, why this distressing
Mingling of death-like agony
    With every balm and blessing?

"O lovely Sphinx! Explain to me
    This riddle that puzzles sages.
I've pondered on it hopelessly,
    Alas, for ages and ages."

TWO DREAM SONNETS

Im nächt'gen Traum hab' ich mich selbst geschaut

I dreamed I saw myself puffed up with pride,
　From head to foot, elaborately dressed
　As for a festival: black coat, silk vest:
And my dear love was standing at my side.
I bowed to her and said, "Are you the bride?
　Congratulations – ah – my very best!"
　Yet something clutched my quivering throat, repressed
The formal sounds until they choked and died.

And then the sound of weeping filled my ears;
　It was my love. Her pale, unhappy face
Almost dissolved in a great wave of tears.
Oh, innocent eyes, love's holy stars, deceive
　Me once again, whate'er the time or place,
Sleeping or waking. I would still believe!

Im Traum sah ich ein Männchen, klein und putzig

I dreamed I saw a dwarf in dapper clothing,
　Who walked on stilts, each step an ell or more.
　Sported white linen – but the stuff he wore
Was black inside: one saw the dirt with loathing.

Within he was all sham; a fuss and frothing
    To draw attention from the rotting core.
    He talked of being brave, and was a bore.
His courage was all cant, and came to nothing.

"And do you know that man, or can you guess?"
    The Dream-god asked me; and he showed me then
    A picture of a church. And of all men
The dwarf was at the altar, nothing less,
My love beside him. Both were saying "Yes!"
    And twice a thousand devils laughed "Amen!"

SONGS

Einsam klag' ich meine Leiden

Lonely now, I pour my sadness
    In the hidden lap of night,
Far from every human gladness,
    Far from men and their delight.

All alone, my tears are flowing,
    Flowing softly, flowing still;
But the heart's too-fiery glowing
    No amount of tears can chill.

YOUTHFUL SORROWS

As a boy, a merry, thieving
  Youngster playing games alone,
Carefree with the joy of living,
  Sorrow was a thing unknown.

Then the world was one great garden
  Made for me, whate'er I chose;
And my labor was as warden
  Of the violet and the rose.

Golden skies and emerald grasses,
  And the sapphire brook flowed by.
Now, although the same brook passes,
  Pale's the picture meets my eye.

Pale am I, too, so they tell me,
  Since she wrought the deadly change.
Secret sorrows overwhelm me;
  Everything is sad and strange.

Once I felt a hushed assembling
  As of angels in my heart;
Now there's turbulence and, trembling,
  All the wings of peace depart.

Night, a blacker night, is falling;
  Shadows threaten, monstrous grown;
In my breast a voice is calling —
  And the voice is not my own.

YOUTHFUL SORROWS

Flames too frightful to believe in
  Shoot through veins like evil wine,
And my very bowels are riven
  With a fire that is not mine.

The dark voice, the unresting fire,
  These unholy flames that run
Through my heart till I expire –
  This, my love, this you have done!

Wenn ich bei meiner Liebsten bin

When I am with my own adored,
  Oh, then my heart beats high;
I am as rich as any lord;
  The world is mine to buy!

But every time I leave her, then
  My wealth, that seemed secure,
Is spent; and I am once again
  The poorest of the poor.

Morgens steh' ich auf und frage

Mornings I arise and wonder
  Will she come today?
Evening passes, still I ponder;
  Still she stays away.

YOUTHFUL SORROWS
~~~~~~~~~~~~~~~

In the night with heavy cumber
    Sleeplessly I lie;
And half dreaming, half in slumber,
    All my days go by.

Es treibt mich hin, es treibt mich her!

It drives me here, it drives me there;
    Soon, in an hour or two, I shall meet her,
    Yes, she herself, and what else could be sweeter –
Heart of mine, why are you throbbing with care?

The hours are such a lazy lot!
    Creeping along with one foot dragging,
    Going the rounds, yawning and lagging –
Come, stir yourselves, you lazy-bones!

Now I am seized with the madness of speed.
    Oh, but they never were lovers, these hours;
    Banded together with hideous powers
They mock at the lover's unrest and his need.

Ich wandelte unter den Bäumen

Wandering under dark branches,
   Alone with my despair,
Touched with a host of memories,
   I started dreaming there.

"Who taught you that word, oh, you songsters,
   You linnets that circle and soar?
Oh, cease, for whenever I hear it
   My heart is tormented once more."

"A girl came singing it always;
   From her own lips we heard,
And all of us birds recaptured
   That lovely, golden word."

"Oh, how can you tell such a story,
  You birds, so sagacious and sly;
You also would capture my sorrows –
  But I will trust no one, not I."

Lieb Liebchen, leg's Händchen aufs Herze mein

My love, lay your hand on my heart in its gloom.
Do you hear that! Like tapping inside of a room!
A carpenter lives there. With malice and glee
He's building a coffin, a coffin for me.

He hammers and pounds with such fiendish delight
I never can sleep, neither daytime nor night,
Oh, carpenter, hurry the hours that creep;
Come, finish your labors – and then I can sleep.

Ich wollte, meine Lieder

I wish that all my love-songs
  Were flowers bright and rare;
I'd send them to my dearest
  And she might find them fair.

I wish that all my love-songs
  Were kisses that could speak;
I'd send them to my dearest
  To hang about her cheek.

I wish that these, my love-songs,
  Were peas, so firm and fat;
I'd make a nice, rich pea-soup –
  And she would relish *that*!

Schöne Wiege meiner Leiden

Lovely cradle of my sorrow,
  Lovely tomb where peace might dwell,
Smiling town, we part tomorrow.
  I must leave; and so, farewell.

Farewell, threshold, where still slowly
  Her beloved footstep stirs;
Farewell to that hushed and holy
  Spot where first my eyes met hers.

Had you never caught or claimed me,
  Fairest, heart's elected queen,
Wretchedness would not have maimed me
  In its toils, as I have been.

Never have you found me grieving
  For your love with anxious prayer;
All I asked was quiet living,
  Quietly to breathe your air.

But you drove me forth with scourging
   Bitter words and lashing scorn;
Madness in my soul is surging,
   And my heart is flayed and torn.

So I take my staff and stumble
   On a journey, far from brave,
Till my head droops, and I tumble
   In some cool and kindly grave.

Berg' und Burgen schaun herunter

Hill and hall are mirrored brightly
   In the clear glass of the Rhine;
And my little ship sails lightly
   Where the sunlit waters shine.

Quietly I watch the shaken,
   Golden billows at their play;
And the thought still comes to waken
   What I hoped was laid away.

For the stream leaps to enamor
   With its warm and laughing light;
Yet I know, for all its glamor,
   Death is in its heart, and night.

Stream, you are her own reflection:
  She can also smile and sin.
She, like you, is all affection:
  Fair outside, and false within.

Anfangs wollt' ich fast verzagen

I despaired at first, declaring
  It could not be borne; and now –
Now I bear it, still despairing.
  Only never ask me how!

Mit Rosen, Cypressen und Flittergold

With rose and with cypress, with tinsel and gold,
This book I'd embellish, brilliant and bold,
Like a royal casket to make men stare,
And all my songs would be buried there.

Could I bury my love, ah, that would be best!
On the grave of love grows the flower of rest.
Others may gather the blossom, not I.
'Twill bloom for me only when buried I lie.

Here, then, are the poems, impulsive and hot
As the lava-streams which from Aetna shot,
Hurled from the depths, leaving many a gash,
With the living flame of a lightning-flash.

Now, cold as corpses, they lie on their bier,
With fixed, hollow eyes, lackluster, here.
Yet swiftly the blood would leap and flow
If love were to breathe on them, set them aglow.

Now in my heart there are whispers that pray
Love may weep over these lyrics some day.
Some day this book may come into your hand,
My own dear love, in a distant land.

And on that day love will sunder the spell;
The cold, dead letters will live and be well.
Your eyes will revive them; the words will move
With the breath and the pain and the longing of love.

Wenn junge Herzen brechen

When young hearts break with passion
    The stars break into laughter,
They laugh and, in their fashion,
    Gossip a long time after:

"Poor souls, those mortals languish
    With love; 'tis all they cherish.
It pays them back with anguish
    And pain until they perish."

"We never can discover
  This love, so brief and breathless,
So fatal to each lover –
  And hence we stars are deathless."

Die Wälder und Felder grünen

There's green on meadow and river;
  The lark seeks a loftier height;
And spring has come in with a quiver
  Of perfume and color and light.

The lark's song has opened the prison
  Of winter-moods, stubborn and strong;
Yet out of my heart has arisen
  A fragment of sorrowful song.

The lark's all a-twitter and cheery:
  "Oh, what makes your singing so drear?"
The song is an old one, my dearie,
  I've sung it for many a year.

'Tis the very same ballad, no other,
  With its burden of sorrowful rhymes –
Why, darling, your own grandmother
  Has heard it a score of times!

17

Ich dacht' an sie den ganzen Tag

I thought about her all the day,
  I thought about her half the night,
And then, while fast asleep I lay,
  A dream disclosed her to my sight.

Like a young rose her color came,
  Sitting so quietly at peace;
She held a small embroidery frame
  Worked in young lambs with virgin fleece.

She looked at me to no avail;
  Why I was there she did not know.
"What makes your face so drawn and pale?
  Heinrich, tell me what hurts you so?"

She looked so tenderly that I
  Trembled; the tears began to flow.
"Why do you weep so hard? And why
  Are you in pain? Who hurts you so?"

She looked so mild, so much at rest,
  My words leaped like an angry blow:
"The pain, my dear, is in my breast;
  You are the one who hurts me so."

Then she stood up and laid her hand
 Upon my heart; like a release
The suffering ceased at her command,
 And once again I was at peace.

Dass ich dich liebe, o Möpschen

I love you, little Mopser;
 You seem to understand.
For when I feed you sugar
 You always lick my hand.

A dog you are, a dog who
 Conducts himself as such.
All of my other friends, alas,
 Disguise themselves too much.

YOUTHFUL SORROWS

~~~~~~~~~~~~~~~~~

Gewiss, gewiss, der Rat war gut

Certainly the advice was good.
But ours was young and eager blood.
We poured, we drank till we were dumb;
We knocked, and someone answered, "Come!"

If, here and there, a fair one frowned,
We knew where kisses could be found.
And when the glass was drained of wine,
Well – grapes still grow along the Rhine.

Du warst ein blondes Jungfräulein, so artig

You were a maiden, blonde, without a flaw,
Perfect and prim. I stayed, but never saw
The hour when you (fond, foolish expectation!)
Opened your heart to any inspiration –

To inspiration for one noble thing
Of which not only poets dare to sing,
But simple certainties the whole world yearns for,
And mankind somehow suffers, bleeds, and burns for.

There was a day I won't forget along the Rhine:
The hills were heavy with the terraced vine.
We walked. The sun laughed; gulls were soaring;
Out of each flower's heart warm scent was pouring.

YOUTHFUL SORROWS

Roses and pinks, confessing their desire,
Sent forth red kisses, little jets of fire;
Even the daisy's gold held brighter plunder,
And every wayside weed was touched with wonder.

But you, in your white dress, walked on with me,
So careful of yourself, so properly;
Neat as a Netcher painting, pink and nice –
Beneath your stays, a little heart of ice.

NARRATIVES

~~~~~~~~~~~~~~~~~~~~~

POOR PETER

Der Hans und die Grete tanzen herum

Oh, Hansel and Gretel are dancing around,
There's shouting and clapping of hands there.
But Peter looks on with never a sound,
And, paler than chalk, he stands there.

For Hansel and Gretel are bridegroom and bride,
Around them the radiance lingers.
But Peter, in workaday clothes, turns aside;
He mutters, and bites his fingers.

Poor Peter still gazes; his grief is intense;
And, watching the pair, he starts sighing:
"Oh, were it not for my good, common sense
I'd end all my sorrows by dying."

"In meiner Brust, da sitzt ein Weh"

"Within my breast there's such a woe
     That I am torn asunder.
  It aches, and though I stay or go
     It drives me always yonder.

"It drives me to my love; it cries
     As though she still could heal me.
  Alas, one look from Gretel's eyes
     And I must fly, conceal me.

"I climb the mountain's highest peak:
     Man is, at least, alone there;
  Where is all still and none may seek,
     My heart may weep and moan there."

Der arme Peter wankt vorbei

Poor Peter, he goes stumbling by
As pale as lead, ashamed and shy.
And all the people stand and stare
Whenever Peter passes there.

The girls all whisper, "Give him room;
He must have risen from the tomb."
Ah, no, my dears, your pity save;
He's only going to his grave.

He's lost his love, his future's dim,
And so the grave's the place for him;
For there his tortured spirit may
Await in peace the Judgment Day.

THE PRISONER'S SONG

Als meine Grossmutter die Liese behext

When grandma bewitched little Lisa, 'twas rich,
  For magic was just her obsession;
Though everyone cried, "Let's burn the old witch!"
  She never would make a confession.

Yet when the flames leaped and the caldron was hot,
  She screamed and she yelled bloody murder;
Then she turned to a raven right there on the spot
  And croaked, although nobody heard her.

Come back, little black-feathered grandmother dear,
  Come, visit me down in this dungeon.
Come, fly through the grating that keeps me in here,
  And bring cheese and cake for my luncheon.

Come back, little black-feathered grandmother! Rise
  And save me from more than my sorrow.
Let none of your relatives pick out my eyes
  When I swing on the gallows tomorrow.

NARRATIVES

THE MESSAGE

Mein Knecht! Steh auf und sattle schnell

My page, arise, and quickly mount
   The horse of swiftest stride;
And breathlessly, through wood and field,
   To Duncan's palace ride.

Wait softly in the stable there
   Until you are espied;
Then ask, "Which one of Duncan's girls
   Is going to be a bride?"

And if they say, "The dark-haired one,"
   Then rush home like the blast.
But if they say, "The light-haired one,"
   You need not ride so fast.

But in the village buy a rope,
   A rope with toughened strands.
Then ride back slowly, speak no word,
   And place it in my hands.

THE GRENADIERS

Nach Frankreich zogen zwei Grenadier'

Toward France there wandered two grenadiers;
  In Russia they had been taken.
And as they reached the German frontiers,
  Body and spirit were shaken.

For there they learned the tragic tale
  That France had been lost and forsaken;
The Army had suffered to no avail,
  And the Emperor, the Emperor was taken!

They wept together, those two grenadiers;
  To one thing their thoughts kept returning.
"Alas," said one, half choked with tears,
  "That old wound of mine keeps burning."

The other said, "This is the end;
　　With you I'd gladly perish.
But there's the homeland to defend,
　　And wife and child to cherish."

"What matters wife? What matters child?
　　With far greater cares I am shaken.
Let them go and beg with hunger wild.
　　My Emperor, my Emperor is taken!

"And, brother, this my only prayer,
　　Now I am dying, grant me:
You'll bear my body to France, and there
　　In the soil of France you'll plant me.

"The cross of honor with crimson band
　　Lay on my heart that bound me;
Then put the musket in my hand
　　And strap my saber round me.

"Then I will lie and listen and wait,
　　A sentinel, down in the grass there,
Till I hear the roar of the guns and the great
　　Thunder of hoofs as they pass there.

"The Emperor will come and the columns will wave;
　　The swords will be flashing and rending;
And I will arise, full-armed, from the grave,
　　My Emperor, my Emperor defending!"

BELSHAZZAR

Die Mitternacht zog näher schon

The noon of night was drawing on;
Dark silence lay on Babylon.

But in the castle of the King
Were flaring lights and reveling;

There, in the royal banquet hall,
Belshazzar held high festival.

He saw his brilliant court recline
And empty bowl on bowl of wine.

He heard cups ring and vassals sing,
And all the brawling pleased the King.

The wine awoke and made him bold:
He flushed; his words grew uncontrolled.

Wine was his passion, wine his prod;
With obscene oaths he mocked at God.

He blasphemed Heaven and all its laws;
The wild court echoed with applause.

The King commanded, his brow was black;
The servant vanished, but hurried back,

Carrying treasures, rich and rare.
The spoil of Jehovah's Temple was there.

The King laid hands on a sacred cup;
With a lewd laugh he filled it up.

He drained the goblet in one quick draught,
And then, with slobbering lips, he laughed:

"Jehovah! I drink to your greatness gone:
I am the King of Babylon!"

The blasphemous words had scarce been said
When something struck the King with dread.

The ribald laugh died in the hall;
Silence fell like a deathly pall;

While on the white wall there appeared
A human hand, abrupt and weird,

And wrote in letters of red flame,
And wrote, and vanished the way it came.

The King's pale features seemed to freeze;
He could not quiet his knocking knees.

Stone-cold about him his courtiers were;
They gave no sound, they made no stir.

Magicians came, yet none of all
Could read that writing upon the wall.

And in the night, death came to one
Belshazzar, King of Babylon.

THE MINNESINGERS

Zu dem Wettgesange schreiten

Come the minnesingers, raising
   Dust and laughter and lament.
Here's a contest that's amazing;
   Here's a curious tournament.

Wild and ever restless Fancy
   Is the minnesinger's horse,
Art his shield, the Word his lance; he
   Bears them lightly round the course.

Many women pleased and pleasant,
   Smile and drop a flower down;
But the right one's never present
   With the cherished laurel-crown.

Other fighters nimbly canter
    To the lists, carefree and whole;
But we minnesingers enter
    With a death-wound in our soul.

And the one who wrings the inmost
    Song-blood from his burning breast,
He's the victor; he shall win most
    Praise and smiles and all the rest.

THE WOUNDED KNIGHT

Ich weiss eine alte Kunde

I know an old, old story;
    Sad is the sound thereof:
A knight lies worn and wounded
    With grief for a faithless love.

He knows she is faithless and scorns her,
    Yet hangs on her wretchedly;
He knows his passion is shameful,
    Yet knows it is stronger than he.

He longs to ride to the tourney
    And shout with a challenging stir,
"Let him prepare for the death-blow
    Who finds a blemish in her!"

But well he knows there'd be silence
    From all save his own unrest;
And his own lance would have to be leveled
    At his loud and accusing breast.

DIALOG ON PADERBORN HEATH

Hörst du nicht die fernen Töne

Do you hear the dim and sprightly
    Sounds of double-bass and fiddle?
Fair ones must be dancing, lightly
    Swinging up and down the middle.

"My poor friend, you are mistaken.
    Fiddles? Fiddlesticks! The squeaking
Comes from living pork and bacon;
    Piglings grunting, sows a-shrieking."

Did you hear those bugles blazing
    As the hunt swept through the forest?
Did you see the lambkins grazing
    While the shepherds' wood-winds chorused?

"Bugles? Wood-winds? These are words, man!
    Neither shepherds roamed, nor hunters.
It was nothing but the herdsman
    Driving home his pack of grunters."

Do you hear far spirits voicing
 Beauty unsurpassed, inspiring?
Angels clap their wings, rejoicing
 To applaud such heavenly choiring.

"Spirits? Angels? What's the use, boy,
 Of such fancies? Far from pious,
That was just a singing goose-boy
 And his geese that wandered by us."

Surely, bells are now in motion;
 And from acres green with tillage
People walk in strict devotion
 To the chapel in the village.

"Nonsense, man! Those are the lowing
 Oxen and the bells of cattle
Plodding through the darkness, going
 To their stalls of mud and wattle."

And that veil, those soft, commanding
 Gestures – say, are those not real?
There my own true love is standing;
 There she waits, the lone ideal.

"She who teases you so much is
 None else but that poor old shadow,
Lisa, on her worn-out crutches,
 Limping slowly through the meadow."

Well then, friend, continue chaffing;
    I confess to the confusion.
Take my dreams; destroy them, laughing.
    Is my heart, too, an illusion?

ABSOLUTELY!

Wenn der Frühling kommt mit dem Sonnenschein

When the spring comes in and the sun is bright,
Then every small blossom beckons and blows.
When the moon on her shining journey goes,
Then stars swim after her through the night.
When the singer looks into two clear eyes,
Then something is stirred and lyrics arise...
But flowers and stars and songs just begun,
And moonbeams and eyes and the light of the sun,
No matter how much such stuff may please,
One can't keep living on things like these.

SONNET TO MY MOTHER

Ich bin's gewohnt den Kopf recht hoch zu tragen

Stubborn and proud, I carry my head high;
Haughty by birth, inflexible in mood,
I would not bow to any king, I would
Not even veil my candid gaze, not I.

But, mother, never let me dare deny
How soon my pride, my boastful hardihood,
Shamed by your presence and solicitude,
Leaves me, without one small departing sigh.

Is it your spirit that o'ermasters me,
Your lofty, penetrating soul that clears
The earth, and cleaves to Heaven, flying free?
Memory burns and rankles, for I know
How often I have brought your heart to tears,
That soft and suffering heart that loved me so.

LYRICAL INTERMEZZO

Meine Qual und meine Klagen

All my anguish, all my rages,
    I have poured and nought concealed here;
And, if you should turn these pages,
    You will find my heart revealed here.

Es war mal ein Ritter, trübselig und stumm

There once was a knight full of sorrow and doubt,
    With cheeks white as snow; indecision
Would lead him to stumble and stagger about
    As though he were trailing a vision.

And he was so wooden, so awkward and dumb
That flowers and maidens, whene'er he would come,
  Would watch him, and laugh in derision.

And often he'd sit in his gloom-shrouded place
  (From men and their joys he had broken),
Stretching thin arms in a yearning embrace,
  Though never a word would be spoken.
But just as the hours to midnight now ran,
A marvelous singing and ringing began,
  With a knock at his door for a token.

And lo, his love enters – a zephyr that blows.
  Of shimmering sea-foam her dress is.
She glows till she grows like the bud of a rose;
  Her veil gleams with gems, and her tresses
Fall to her feet in a golden array;
Her eyes are impassioned. The lovers give way
  And yield to each other's caresses.

He holds her so close that his heart almost breaks.
  The wooden one now is afire;
The pallid one reddens, the dreamer awakes,
  The bashful is bold with desire.
But she, she coquettes and she teases, and then
With her magical veil she must bind him again,
  Who blindly can only admire.

In a watery palace of crystalline light
   She has 'witched him, and all that was bitter
Turns golden and fair, all is suddenly bright;
   His eyes are bemused with the glitter.
The nixie still presses him close to her side;
The knight is the bridegroom, the nixie the bride–
   Her maidens keep playing the zither.

Oh, sweetly they sing and sweetly they play;
   Fair feet in the dances are shown there;
The knight in his ardor is swooning away
   And tighter he clasps her, his own there...
Then all in an instant is plunged into gloom,
And our hero is sitting once more in his room.
   In his poet's dim garret, alone there!

Im wunderschönen Monat Mai

In May, the magic month of May,
   When every bud was springing,
My heart was filled with fervors,
   With dreams of young love clinging.

In May, the magic month of May,
   When every bird was singing,
I poured out all the rapture
   With which my heart was ringing.

Aus meinen Tränen spriessen

Out of my tears and sorrows
   The blossoming flowers arise,
And nightingales in choir
   Are born of all my sighs.

Dear child, if you would love me
   Those flowers to you I'd bring;
And here before your window
   The nightingales would sing.

Die Rose, die Lilie, die Taube, die Sonne

The rose and the lily, the dove and the sun,
I loved them all once, before love had begun.
I love them no more. I worship now solely
The one and the only most holy and lowly.
She, herself, is the spirit of all these in one;
Being Rose and the Lily, the Dove and the Sun.

Wenn ich in deine Augen seh'

Whene'er I look into your eyes
Then all my grief and sorrow flies;
And when I kiss your mouth, oh, then
I am made well and strong again.

And when I lean upon your breast
My soul is soothed with godlike rest;
But when you say, "I love you," see
How I must weep, how bitterly!

Dein Angesicht, so lieb und schön

Your face has grown so dear, it seems
A vision only seen in dreams;
So seraph-like, so mild and frail,
And still so pale, so sadly pale.

Only your lips are red, and they
Soon kissed by death turn cold and gray;
And dimmed will be the azure skies
That lie within those candid eyes.

Lehn deine Wang' an meine Wang'

Oh, lean your cheek against my cheek,
  Our tears thus shall mingle and flow, love.
And to my heart press close your heart,
  The flames beating so, love, shall glow, love.

And when the leaping radiance glows
  With tears like torrents thronging,
And when my arms are enfolding you close,
  I die of love, and longing.

Ich will meine Seele tauchen

I will baptize my spirit
 In the lily's glowing core;
The lily shall tremble and hear it,
 A song of the one I adore.

That song shall live and have me
 Thrilled with a subtle power,
Like the kiss that once she gave me
 In a pure and poignant hour.

Es stehen unbeweglich

Immovable for ages
 The stars are set above;
They look upon each other
 With all the pain of love.

And, oh, they speak a language,
 So wondrous, each to each,
That not the wisest scholar
 Can understand their speech.

But I have learned it, and never
 Can I hear it again unmoved;
For lo, I used as a grammar
 The face of my beloved!

Auf Flügeln des Gesanges

On wings of song, my dearest,
   I will carry you off, and go
To where the Ganges is clearest;
   There is a haven I know.

In the moonlight's glow and glister
   Fair gardens radiate;
Eager to greet their sister,
   The lotus-flowers wait.

Violets tease one another
   And gaze at the stars from the vales;
Roses are telling each other,
   Secretly, sweet-scented tales.

And lightly, trespassing slowly,
   Come the placid, timid gazelles;
Far in the distance, the holy
   River rises and swells.

Oh, that we two were by it!
   Beneath a palm by the stream.
To drink in love and quiet,
   And dream a peaceful dream.

Die Lotosblume ängstigt

The lotus-blossom cowers
  Under the sun's bright beams;
Her forehead drooping for hours,
  She waits for the night among dreams.

The moon, he is her lover,
  He wakes her with his gaze;
To him alone she uncovers
  The fair flower of her face.

She glows and grows more radiant,
  And gazes mutely above;
Breathing and weeping and trembling
  With love – and the pain of love.

Im Rhein, im schönen Strome

In the Rhine, that stream of wonder,
  The great, the holy Cologne
Is mirrored, and there under
  The waves the Cathedral is shown.

The Cathedral has within it
  A portrait done in gold;
And, in my wild life's sin, it
  Has taken a wondrous hold.

44

'Mid flowers and angels she stands there,
    Our Lady we bow before,
But the eyes and the lips and the hands there
    Are those of the one I adore!

Du liebst mich nicht, du liebst mich nicht

You love me not, you love me not.
    Oh, that's a trivial thing.
For when I see your face, my lot
    Is that of any king.

You hate me, hate me – even this.
    Your red lips dare declare it!
    Well, let me have those lips to kiss,
And I, my child, can bear it.

Du sollst mich liebend umschliessen

O come, love, now I resign me;
    I yield myself to your charms.
O come, that you may intertwine me
    With the tenderest, supplest of arms.

And winding thus and wounding,
    Embracing and crushing, is shown
The fairest of serpents surrounding
    The happiest Laocoön.

O schwöre nicht und küsse nur

O kiss me, love, and never swear,
For women's oaths are light as air.
Your speech is sweet, but sweeter is
The perfect silence of your kiss.
'Tis this alone that has my faith —
The word is but a perfumed breath.

Well, swear then, love; oh, swear away;
I will believe each word you say.
And as I sink upon your breast
I will believe that I am blessed;
I will believe your love of me
Stretches beyond eternity.

Auf meiner Herzliebsten Äugelein

Upon my dearest's little eyes
    I make the best *canzoni*.
Upon her mouth, so small in size,
    The best of *terza rima*.
Upon my darling's cheeks, likewise
    I make the loveliest stanzas.
And if she had a heart, upon it
    I'd make a really charming sonnet.

Die Welt ist dumm, die Welt ist blind

The world is dull, the world is blind.
　　Each day more of a mad one.
It says, my dear, that, to its mind,
　　Your character's a bad one.

The world is dull, the world is blind.
　　Its dullness is really distressing;
It does not know that your kisses are kind,
　　And that they can burn with their blessing.

Liebste, sollst mir heute sagen

Come, and you shall tell me, dearest,
　　Are you not a thing of dreams,
Such as, when the summer's clearest,
　　From the poet's fancy streams?

47

Ah, but no, a mien so mild, dear,
    Such a mouth and eyes that wait,
Such a loving, lovely child, dear,
    Not a poet could create.

Basilisks whose glances freeze or
    Hippogriffs and dragons dire;
Horrid, fabled things like these are
    Fashioned in the poet's fire.

But yourself and your pretenses,
    And those eyes that could not hate –
And those false and fervent glances
    Not a poet could create.

Wie die Wellenschaumgeborene

Like the Foam-born, my love glows in
    Splendor and her beauty's pride,
For she is the happy chosen
    One to be a stranger's bride.

Though this treason may be hard on
    You, my heart, poor patient one;
Bear it, beat it still, and pardon
    What the pretty fool has done.

LYRICAL INTERMEZZO

Ich grolle nicht, und wenn das Herz auch bricht

I will not mourn, although my heart is torn,
Oh, love forever lost! I will not mourn.
Although tricked out in white and diamond light,
No single ray falls in thy heart's deep night.

I know this well . . . I saw thee in a dream
And saw the night within thy heart supreme;
And saw the snake that gnawed upon thy heart.
I saw how wretched, oh, my love, thou art.

Ja, du bist elend, und ich grolle nicht

Yes, you are wretched, and I do not mourn –
    Wretched, my love, it seems we both must be.
Until in death the weary heart is torn,
    Wretched, my love, it seems we both must be.

I see the twisted, scornful mouth; the wide
    Defiance in the sudden-blazing eye;
I see the bosom heave with angry pride.
    Yes, you are wretched, wretched even as I.

Your lips contract with unseen thrusts of pain;
    The tears are hidden; but adversity
Stabs the proud breast again and yet again –
    Wretched, my love, it seems we both must be.

Das ist ein Flöten und Geigen

The violins are shrilling;
   The trumpets blaze and blare;
The wedding-music is thrilling;
   My love is dancing there.

With what a droning and groaning
   The drums and reeds are rent;
While, sobbing and bemoaning,
   The cherubim lament.

So hast du ganz und gar vergessen

So now you have forgotten wholly
How once your heart was mine, mine solely;
Your heart had so sweet and so false a glow,
Nothing is sweeter or falser, I know.

So the love and the pain are forgotten wholly
That tortured my heart and made it lowly,
But whether the pain was as great as my love,
I know not. I know they were both great enough.

Und wüssten's die Blumen, die kleinen

And were it known to the flowers
  How wounded my heart must be,
Their tears would fall in showers
  To heal my agony.

If nightingale and linnet
  Knew of my sadness and pain,
Their singing would have in it
  A far more joyful strain.

If sorrow's tearful traces
  The golden stars could see,
They would come down from their places
  And try to comfort me.

But they cannot comprehend it—
  One, only, knows my pain;
She took my heart to rend it
  Again and yet again.

Warum sind denn die Rosen so blass

Oh, why are all the roses so pale,
  My love, come tell me why?
Oh, why, in fields that could not fail,
  Do violets droop and die?

Oh, why, to the sound of so doleful a lute,
    Do linnets lift their wings?
Oh, why does there spring from each fragrant root
    The odor of dead things?

Oh, why does the sun send so dreary a ray
    Over fields where he shone so brave?
Oh, why is all of the earth as gray
    And desolate as a grave?

And I, myself, am so troubled and weak;
    My love, why should this be?
Answer, my own; my lost darling, speak –
    Why have you done this to me?

Sie haben dir viel erzählet

They have told you many stories
    And made a great to-do;
But why my spirit worries
    Has not been told to you.

They made such a stir and pother,
    Complained of the life I led;
"A devil!" they said to each other;
    And you believed all they said.

And yet the very worst thing
 They never have even guessed;
For the worst and most accurst thing,
 I carry hid in my breast.

Die Linde blühte, die Nachtigall sang

The linden blossomed, the nightingale sang,
 The great sun laughed with a friendly light;
You kissed me, my love, and the while my heart sprang,
 To your palpitant bosom you folded me tight.

The raven screamed harshly, the withered leaves fell,
 The sun's cold greeting was sharpened with spite;
We beckoned each other a frosty farewell,
 And politely you curtsied a curtsey polite.

Wir haben viel für einander gefühlt

How deep we were wrapped in each other's life,
How well we behaved (and how bitter the moral);
How often we played at man and wife,
With never a blow or the sign of a quarrel.
We sported together in joy and in jest
And tenderly kissed and sweetly caressed
And finally playing, like children that go,
At hide and seek in the woodland together;

We managed to stray and hide ourselves so
That each of us now is lost to the other.

Ich glaub' nicht an den Himmel

I have no faith in Heaven
    Of which the preachers write;
Your eyes I do believe in –
    They are my heavenly light.

I have no faith in Godhead
    Of which the preachers read;
Your heart I do believe in –
    No other God I need.

I have no faith in Satan,
    In Hell and Hell's fierce smart;
Your eyes I do believe in –
    And in your wicked heart.

LYRICAL INTERMEZZO

~~~~~~~~~~~~~~~

Du bleibest mir treu am längsten

You were steadfast and true the longest;
   Your care you always gave me,
   Your thought would cheer and save me
When fear and need were strongest.

A gift of gold would not grieve you,
   And food you ne'er denied me;
   With linen you supplied me
Whene'er I had to leave you.

And for this great amount, He,
   The Lord, I pray will be tender
   To you and reward the splendor
Of your amazing bounty.

Die Erde war so lange geizig

The earth kept hoarding up its treasure;
   Man spent it to a mighty babel
Of all that laughed and voiced its pleasure –
   But I, I find I am not able.

The bells' and flowers' speech reprove me,
   The birds converse as in the fable;
But all these wonders do not move me,
   For life is sad, and joy unstable.

Man bores me, even as the merest
   Gossip of friends about the table –
Because she is no longer "dearest,"
   But "Madam"... Hence my soul wears sable.

Und als ich so lange, so lange gesäumt

And thus, as I wasted many a day
In wandering and dreaming the hours away,
My love found the waiting too long a recess,
She started to sew on her wedding-dress;
And caught in her arms (oh, deluded and dupèd)
As husband, the stupidest one of the stupid.

My loved one is so mild and fair,
Her likeness haunts me everywhere;
The rose-cheeks and the violet-eyes
Year in, year out, their ghosts arise.
And that I should lose a love so dear,
Was the stupidest act of my stupid career.

Die blauen Veilchen der Äugelein

The violets blue which are her eyes,
The crimson rose which her cheek outvies,
The lilies white which her hands disguise,
These blossom and glow; they never fade.
It's only the heart that has decayed.

LYRICAL INTERMEZZO

Die Welt ist so schön und der Himmel so blau

The world is so fair and the heaven so blue
And the breezes so mild that come whispering through,
And the flowers arise on the roadside anew,
And glisten and gleam in the morning dew,
And mankind is happy, whatever the view –
But still I would lie in the grave uncherished
With only the ghost of a love that has perished.

Mein süsses Lieb, wenn du im Grab

Love, when you sink where darkness lies
    Before you and behind you,
I shall go down with all that dies
    And seek you out – and find you.

I'll clasp you with kisses, burning and wild,
    So pale, so unmoved, and so cold there.
Trembling and weeping, rejoicing and mild
    I will grow like a corpse and mold there.

The dead stand up as midnight calls;
    They dance thro' airy spaces.
We two will remain, wrapped in our palls,
    Secure in our embraces.

The dead stand up; the Judgment Day
　　Calls them to pain or pleasure.
But we will dream the hours away
　　Together at our leisure.

Ein Fichtenbaum steht einsam

A lonely pine is standing
　　In the North where high winds blow.
He sleeps; and the whitest blanket
　　Wraps him in ice and snow.

He dreams – dreams of a palm-tree
　　That far in an Eastern land
Languishes, lonely and drooping,
　　Upon the burning sand.

Schöne, helle, goldne Sterne

Stars, with fair and golden ray,
Greet my loved one far away;
Say that I still wear the rue,
Sick at heart and pale – and true.

Ach, wenn ich nur der Schemel wär'

THE HEAD SPEAKS:

Oh, were I but the stool that she
 Uses to rest her feet from pain;
Yes, though she stamped and trod on me,
 I would not murmur or complain.

THE HEART SPEAKS:

Oh, were I but the cushion, too,
 That holds the needle she employs;
Yes, though she pierced me through and through,
 Each stab would wake the wildest joys.

THE SONG SPEAKS:

Oh, were I but the least – the mere
 Paper with which she curls her hair!
Then would I whisper in her ear
 What stirs in me, and all I dare.

Seit die Liebste war entfernt

 Since, my love, we had to part
 Laughter died within my heart.
 Many jesters quip and quaff;
 But I cannot hope to laugh.

Since my love was lost to me
Weeping also ceased to be.
Broken, tortured, robbed of sleep –
But I cannot even weep.

Aus meinen grossen Schmerzen

From my great grief, I fashion
   The little songs I utter;
   They lift their wings and flutter
Off to her heart with passion.

Over her bosom they hover –
   But soon they fly homeward complaining;
   Complaining but never explaining
What, in her heart, they discover.

Ich kann es nicht vergessen

It will not die, but solely
   This thought comes to condole,
How once I had you wholly,
   Your body and your soul.

Your body still I crave for,
   Your body's lovely growth.
Your soul you may dig a grave for;
   I've soul enough for us both!

I'll cut my spirit in two, dear,
   And breathe in you half of the whole
And clasp you – thus forming anew, dear,
   One perfect body and soul.

Philister im Sonntagsröcklein

Smug burghers and tradesmen are tripping
   Through woods in the smartest style;
Like goats they are hopping and skipping,
   Admiring 'fair Nature' the while.

In eyes that are bleary and blinking
   A ray of romance springs;
And great, long ears are drinking
   The song the sparrow sings.

But I am beclouding and shrouding
   My windows with curtains of gray;
For a host of specters are crowding
   To pay me a visit today.

My old love comes in, creeping
   From death's immense domain;
She sits by my side, and, weeping,
   She melts my heart again.

Manch' Bild vergessener Zeiten

From graves of times forgotten
   Old visions come to me
Revealing what, when near you,
   My life once used to be.

By day I wandered dreaming
   Through streets and alleys until
The people looked at me wondering;
   I was so gloomy and still.

By night it was somewhat better –
   The streets were an empty rout;
And I and my shadow together
   Went staggering blindly about.

~~~~~~~~~~~~~~~~~

With ever-echoing footsteps
   I crossed the bridge by chance;
The moon broke through the darkness
   And shot me an earnest glance.

I stood there, before your dwelling,
   And stared into the night;
Gazing up at your window,
   My heart was torn at the sight.

I know that, from the window,
   Those lonely streets you scanned,
And saw me in the moonbeams,
   Like some white pillar stand.

Ein Jüngling liebt ein Mädchen

A young man loves a maiden,
   Whose heart for another has yearned;
This other loves another
   By whom his love is returned.

The maiden weds in anger
   The first good man she spies
Who runs into her pathway;
   The youth grows bitter and wise.

It is an old, old story
    But one that's always new;
And every time it happens
    It breaks a heart in two.

Freundschaft, Liebe, Stein der Weisen

Friendship, Love, the Philosopher's Stone,
These three things are ranked alone;
These I sought from sun to sun,
And I found – not even one!

Hör' ich das Liedchen klingen

I hear an echo singing
    The song she sang for me;
And a fresh grief is wringing
    My heart's old agony.

A wild unrest is sweeping
    Me where the high woods grow;
There I may lose, through weeping,
    My overburdening woe.

Es schauen die Blumen alle

Now all the flowers are gazing
    At the glowing and radiant sun,
And all of the brooks are seeking
    The heart of the sea as they run.

And all of the songs are flying
    To the most desired and dear –
Take with you my tears and my sorrows,
    Ye songs that are saddened and drear.

Mir träumte von einem Königskind

I dreamed of the daughter of a king;
    With teary, weary faces
We sat beneath a linden's wing,
    Wrapt in each other's embraces.

"I do not want thy father's throne,
    His scepter with gold o'erladen;
I do not want his brilliant crown,
    I want but thee, dear maiden."

"That cannot be," she said to me,
    "For in the grave I am lying,
And only at night I come to thee,
    Because my love is undying."

Mein Liebchen, wir sassen beisammen

My dearest, we nestled devoted,
    Alone in a fairy-like bark.
The night was still; and we floated
    Out on the watery dark.

A spirit-isle we discovered
    In the moonlight's vague expanse;
Where airy music hovered
    And wove in a misty dance.

The sounds were sweet, and gladdened
    The night with their magicry.
But we – we passed it, saddened
    And worn on a widening sea.

Aus alten Märchen winkt es

From ancient fairy-stories
    Beckons an airy hand;
A voice, with hints of glories,
    Sings of a magic land,

Where flowers have fairer blossoms
    In a golden evening's grace,
And bare their fragrant bosoms,
    Lifting a bride-like face.

Where all the trees are voicing
    Their songs, as in a choir;
Where rivers dance, rejoicing,
    And every wind's a lyre.

Where wilder passions quicken,
    Where wilder beauty throngs,
Till you are wonder-stricken
    With wonder-striking songs.

Ah, to be taken yonder
    To let my heart go free;
There in a land of wonder
    How blessèd it would be.

Ah, Land of Pleasant Places,
    Land of a dreamer's dream —
Alas, like foam it passes,
    Swept by a hurrying stream.

Ich hab' dich geliebet und liebe dich noch!

I loved thee once, and I love thee now.
    Though the stars in a golden shower
Should fall, above the chaos and glow
    The flame of my love would tower.

Am leuchtenden Sommermorgen

On a radiant summer morning
 Into the garden I stray;
The flowers rustle and whisper,
 But I have nothing to say.

The flowers whisper and murmur,
 Pleading as only they can:
"Oh, be not wroth with our sister,
 Thou bitter and sorrowful man."

Es leuchtet meine Liebe

My love and its dark magic
 Troubles me with its might,
Like a story, tender and tragic,
 Told on a summer night:

"In an enchanted bower
 Two lovers walk, half-awake;
The moon, like a great white flower,
 Lies on the breast of a lake.

"A picture: the maid almost pliant,
 And on his knees, the knight.
When lo, from the shadows a giant
 Springs, and the maid takes flight.

"The knight sinks bleeding and dying,
  The giant tramps back to his hold..."
When in the grave I am lying
  The rest of the tale will be told.

Sie haben mich gequälet

Many have made me wretched,
  Made mine an evil fate;
Some of them with their loving,
  Some of them with their hate.

My cup has been filled with poison;
  They poisoned the bread I ate;
Some of them with their loving,
  Some of them with their hate.

Yet she, whose poison made me
  Wretched all men above,
Gave me no word of hatred –
  And not a spark of love.

Es liegt der heisse Sommer

The golden flame of summer
  Burns in your glowing cheek;
But in your heart lies winter,
  Barren and cold and bleak.

Soon it will change, my darling,
　　Far sooner than you seek;
Your heart will harbor summer,
　　While winter lines your cheek.

Wenn zwei von einander scheiden

When two who love are parted,
　　They talk, as friend to friend,
Clasp hands and weep a little,
　　And sigh without an end.

We did not weep, my darling,
　　Nor sigh "Why must this be!"
The tears, the sighs, the anguish
　　Came later – and to me.

Sie sassen und tranken am Teetisch

'Twas tea-time; the mildly aesthetic
　　Ensemble took *Love* as their theme.
The mood of the guests was poetic;
　　They gushed like a lyrical stream.

"True love must be always platonic,"
　　A hardened old councilor cried.
With a laugh that was almost ironic,
　　His wife looked upward and sighed.

A canon spoke, "We must resist 'em,
　These pleasures that rouse and harass,
Or else they will ruin the system."
　And a pretty young thing lisped, "Alas."

The countess, drooping and yearning,
　Said, "Love must sweep on like the sea!"
As, elegantly turning,
　She handed the baron his tea.

Still, it was not quite complete, dear;
　Your place stood empty above.
And, oh, it would have been sweet, dear,
　To hear *you* prattle of love.

Vergiftet sind meine Lieder

My songs, you say, are poisoned.
　How else, love, could it be?
You have, with deadly magic,
　Poured poison into me.

My songs, you say, are poisoned.
　And well I know it, too.
I carry a thousand serpents
　And, love, among them – you.

LYRICAL INTERMEZZO

Mir träumte wieder der alte Traum

Again the old dream came to me:
   'Twas May; the world was vernal;
We sat beneath the linden tree
   And pledged a faith eternal.

Great love and a deathless oath we swore.
   And that I might never forget it,
With a passionate kiss and a thousand more
   You took my hand, and bit it.

Oh, sweetheart with the lips that cling,
   With eyes so clear and merry,
The oath was quite the proper thing –
   The bite, unnecessary.

Ich steh' auf des Berges Spitze

I stand on the mountain's summit
   Emotional and absurd.
Sighing these maudlin verses:
   "Would that I were a bird!"

Oh, if I were a swallow
   I'd fly to you for rest,
And, underneath your window,
   I'd build my little nest.

72

And if I were, oh, dearest,
   A splendid nightingale,
All night you'd hear me singing
   From many a verdant vale.

And if I were a jay-bird
   My hopes to you I'd raise;
For you are kind to jay-birds
   And to the call of jays!

Mein Wagen rollet langsam

My carriage rolls on slowly;
   Woods are a cheerful green;
Valleys exult with flowers;
   The world's a magic scene.

73

I sit and think of my loved one,
 And dream she might be here;
And lo, at my side three phantoms
 Curtsey, and grin, and leer.

They bow, and bob, and caper,
 Mocking, yet bashful and kind.
And then, like an eddy of vapor,
 They titter and pass with the wind.

Ich hab' im Traum geweinet

I wept as I lay dreaming,
 I dreamed that you had died.
And, when I woke, the tear-drops
 Clung to my cheeks undried.

I wept as I lay dreaming,
 I dreamed you were false to me.
I woke, and for many hours
 Lay weeping bitterly.

I wept as I lay dreaming,
 I dreamed that your love was true.
I woke, to an endless weeping,
 And the endless thought of you.

Allnächtlich im Traume seh' ich dich

Belovèd, in dreams we often meet,
    And lo, your voice is kindly.
I fling myself at your gracious feet,
    And weep there, long and blindly.

You shake your fair head, sunbeam-swept,
    Reproachful yet appealing,
As out of eyes that never wept
    The blessèd tears come stealing.

You whisper a word for me alone
    And give me a wreath, dream-begotten . . .
I wake. The cypress-wreath is gone,
    And the word is quite forgotten!

Das ist ein Brausen und Heulen

A howling storm is brewing,
    The wind and rain are wild;
And what can my love be doing,
    That pale and frightened child?

There at the window dreaming,
    I see her, worn and white;
With eyes no longer beaming,
    She stares into the night.

ᏴᏴᏴᏴᏴᏴᏴᏴᏴ

Der Herbstwind rüttelt die Bäume

Wild autumn shakes the branches,
    The night is damp and cold;
I ride through a lonely forest,
    Wrapped in my mantle's fold.

And, as I ride, my fancies
    Fly faster along the road;
They bear me, light and eager,
    To her beloved abode.

The dogs awake; the torches
    Flare, and the whole house stirs;
I storm the spiral staircase
    And mount, with a clatter of spurs.

Lo, in her own soft chamber,
    Warm with its fragrant charms,
My love awaits me, smiling –
    I fly to her open arms...

I hear the oak-tree speaking;
    The wind, in the branches, screams:
"What would you, O wild horseman –
    You and your wilder dreams!"

Es fällt ein Stern herunter

A star, a star is falling
    Out of the glittering sky.
The star of love! I watch it
    Sink in the depths and die.

The leaves and buds are falling
    From many an apple-tree;
I watch the mirthful breezes
    Embrace them wantonly.

A swan, a swan is singing;
    I watch it floating by,
As, drooping low and lower,
    The song and singer die.

It is so dark and silent!
    The star that burned so long
Is dust; the leaves are ashes;
    Hushed is the swan's last song.

Der Traumgott bracht' mich in ein Riesenschloss

The Dream-God led me to a castle grim,
    Full of strange lights, strange scents and stranger glamor;
And through great labyrinths there seemed to swim
    Wild multitudes whom nothing could enamor.

77

Onward they swept, through halls and portals dim,
   Wringing pale hands with an incessant clamor.
Maidens and knights I saw among the throng,
And, with the torrent, I was borne along.

When suddenly I am alone – and lo,
   I cannot find a single face whatever.
Through frowning aisles and winding rooms I go;
   Fiercely impelled by one intense endeavor.
But oh, my feet are lead, my footsteps slow
   To find the gate, and leave this place forever.
At last, I gain the portals with a prayer,
Fling wide the door and leap... *O God, who's there!*

My love! Beside that door I saw her stand,
   Pain on her lips and sorrow's crown above her.
Then back she turned me with a waving hand,
   Threatening or warning, I could not discover.
Yet, from her eyes, sprang, like a sweet command,
   A fire that made me once again her lover.
Tender and strong, her very glances spoke
The flaming speech of love – and I awoke.

   Die Mitternacht war kalt und stumm

  'Twas midnight, still and very cold;
   Through the dark woods I sang and strolled.
  I shook the trees with my doleful ditty;
   They only nodded their heads in pity.

Am Kreuzweg wird begraben

They buried him at the cross-roads,
   Whose own hand wrought his doom;
And over him grow blue flowers
   Called the Poor-Sinner's-Bloom.

I stand at the cross-roads sighing,
   Wrapped in a cloak of gloom,
And watch the moonlight trembling
   On the Poor-Sinner's-Bloom.

Wo ich bin, mich rings umdunkelt

Now the night grows deeper, stronger;
　Darkness dense about me lies,
Since the stars died; since no longer,
　Love, can I behold your eyes.

Dimmed, forgotten is the dawning
　Of that great and golden light;
At my feet the pit is yawning.
　Take me – stark, eternal Night.

Nacht lag auf meinen Augen

Night lay upon my eyelids,
　Upon my mouth lay lead;
My heart and brain were barren;
　I lay with all the dead.

How long I lay there sleeping
　I know not; but I gave
A start and turned, for knocking
　Sounded above my grave.

"Rise up, rise up, O Heinrich,
　The dawn eternal breaks,
When all the dead are risen
　And deathless joy awakes."

I cannot rise, my dearest;
    Your face I cannot find.
I've wept until my sorrows
    And tears have made me blind.

"From your dear eyes, O Heinrich,
    I'll kiss the night away;
Then you shall see the angels,
    And Heaven's bright array."

I cannot rise, my dearest,
    Bleeding I lie, unstirred;
Since, to the heart, you stabbed me
    With one short, bitter word.

"Softly I'll lay, O Heinrich,
    My hand upon your heart;
Then it will bleed no longer,
    And I will soothe the smart."

I cannot rise, my dearest,
    My head is bleeding too;
'Tis there I fired the pistol
    The day that I lost you!

"With my own hair, O Heinrich,
    I'll stop the gaping wound,
Press back the streaming torrent,
    And make you strong and sound."

So soft her call, so tender,
　　She could not be denied;
I strove to rend my coffin
　　And struggle to her side.

Then all my wounds burst open;
　　I felt the torrent break
From head and burning bosom...
　　And lo, I was awake!

Die alten bösen Lieder

The songs so old and bitter,
　　The dreams so wild and drear,
Let's bury them together.
　　What ho! A coffin here!

I have so much to bury
　　It never will be done,
Unless the coffin's larger
　　Than Heidelberg's Great Tun.

And bring a bier to match it
　　Of stoutest oaks and pines;
It must be even longer
　　Than the long bridge at Mainz.

82

And also bring twelve giants
    Of mightier brawn and bone
Than Christopher, the sainted,
    Whose shrine is in Cologne.

And in the great sea sink it
    Beneath the proudest wave;
For such a mighty coffin
    Should have a mighty grave.

You know what makes my coffin
    So great, so hard to bear?
It holds my love within it,
    And my too heavy care.

THE HOME-COMING

In mein gar zu dunkles Leben

In my life's too constant darkness
    Once a vision shed its light;
Now, the phantom radiance vanished,
    I am wrapped again in night.

Children, when oppressed by darkness,
    When their happy hearts are cowed,
To allay their fears and trembling
    Sing a song – and sing too loud.

I, a child half-crazed, am singing,
    Singing in the darkness here.
If my song is loud and raucous,
    It, at least, has soothed my fear.

THE HOME-COMING

Ich weiss nicht, was soll es bedeuten

I cannot tell why this imagined
    Despair has fallen on me;
The ghost of an ancient legend
    That will not let me be:

The air is cool, and twilight
    Flows down the quiet Rhine;
A mountain alone in the high light
    Still holds the faltering shine.

The last peak rosily gleaming
    Reveals, enthroned in air,
A maiden, lost in dreaming,
    Who combs her golden hair.

Combing her hair with a golden
    Comb in her rocky bower,
She sings the tune of an olden
    Song that has magical power.

The boatman has heard; it has bound him
    In throes of a strange, wild love.
Blind to the reefs that surround him,
    He sees but the vision above.

And lo, hungry waters are springing –
    Boat and boatman are gone . . . .
Then silence. And this, with her singing,
    The Loreley has done.

Mein Herz, mein Herz ist traurig

My heart is full of sorrow
    Though May is full of cheer;
I stand beside the linden,
    High on the bastion here.

THE HOME-COMING

I watch the blue moat idly;
   Gently it flows along.
A boy in a drifting rowboat
   Angles, and whistles a song.

Beyond, like a quaint, toy village,
   Tiny and many-hued,
Are houses, gardens, and people,
   Oxen, meadow, and wood.

Bleaching their piles of linen
   The girls are frolicsome.
The millwheel spatters diamonds;
   I hear its distant hum.

Upon the old, gray tower
   A sentry-box stands low;
And there a chap in scarlet
   Is pacing to and fro.

He practices with his rifle
   That catches the sunset's red;
He shoulders it and presents it –
   Would that he shot me dead!

THE HOME-COMING

Im Walde wandl' ich und weine

I pace the greenwood, bitter
  With tears, and as I go
A thrush begins to twitter,
  "Why are you sorrowing so?"

Ask of your sisters, the swallows;
  They know, though none of them tells.
They nest in the eaves and hollows
  Where the belovèd dwells.

Die Nacht ist feucht und stürmisch

The night is wet and stormy;
  No stars are in the sky;
The boughs in the forest whisper;
  I wander slowly by.

Far off a candle glimmers
  From the forester's lonely room;
But there the light shall not lure me,
  It is too wrapped in gloom.

The sightless grandmother's sitting
  In the high-backed, leather chair;
She listens, stiff as a statue,
  Uncanny and silent there.

THE HOME-COMING

Cursing and pacing in anger,
   The forester's red-headed son
Laughs in a burst of fury,
   And throws aside his gun.

The girl weeps at her spinning,
   And moistens the flax with her tears.
While at her feet, the dachshund
   Trembles with unknown fears.

Als ich auf der Reise zufällig

By chance I met on the journey
   My dear one's family,
Sister and mother and father;
   Smiling, they greeted me.

How was my health? My spirits?
   They?... Oh, the same old tale.
I hadn't changed much, they told me;
   Only a trifle pale.

I asked about aunts and cousins
   With interest (save the mark!)
And other such pleasing people,
   And the dog, with his gentle bark.

How was my married sweetheart
　Whom they had left behind?
And smilingly they told me
　That she had just been confined.

I coughed congratulations,
　And, stammering wretchedly,
I asked them all to greet her
　A thousand times for me.

Then spoke the little sister:
　"That puppy pet of mine
Grew up so big and horrid
　We drowned him in the Rhine."

The child resembles her sister,
　Sometimes remarkably so;
Those eyes and that way of laughing
　That brought me so much woe.

THE HOME-COMING

Wir sassen am Fischerhause

We sat by the hut of the fisher
   And idly watched the sea,
While in the hush of evening
   The mists rose silently.

The yellow lights in the lighthouse
   Shone like a burnished bell,
And in the hazy distance
   One ship still rose and fell.

We spoke of storm and shipwreck,
   The sailor and his life,
Tossed between sky and water,
   Fierce joy and lusty strife.

We gossiped of distant places,
   Of North and of South we spoke,
Of wild and curious customs,
   And wild and curious folk.

Of how the Ganges sparkles;
   Of great exotic trees;
Of folk who worship the lotus
   Silently, on their knees.

Of Lapland; its slovenly people,
    Flat-headed, broad-featured and small.
That do little else but bake fishes
    And squat by the fire and squall.

The girls all listened breathless;
    Then silence, like a spell.
The ship could be seen no longer –
    Swiftly the darkness fell.

Du schönes Fischermädchen

Oh, lovely fishermaiden,
    Come, bring your boat to land;
And we will sit together
    And whisper, hand in hand.

Oh, rest upon my bosom,
    And fear no harm from me.
You give your body daily,
    Unfearing to the sea.

My heart is like the ocean
    With storm and ebb and flow;
And many a pearly treasure
    Burns in the depths below.

THE HOME-COMING
∿∿∿∿∿∿∿∿∿

Der Mond ist aufgegangen

The yellow moon has risen,
    It slants upon the sea;
And in my arms' soft prison
    My love leans close to me.

Warm with her gentle clinging,
    I lie on the sands, half awake.
"Oh, what do you hear in the swinging
    Of the winds, and why do you shake?"

"That's never the wind that is swinging,
    This murmur that troubles me;
It is the mermaidens singing –
    My sisters drowned in the sea."

Auf den Wolken ruht der Mond

The moon is lying on the clouds,
    A giant orange, strangely beaming;
Stretched upon the harsh gray sea,
    Long and broadening stripes are gleaming.

Alone I wander by the shore
    Where the waters break and whiten,
And I hear a watery voice,
    And my pulses leap and tighten.

93

Oh, the night is far too long
    And I cannot bear this quiet.
Come, ye lovely water-sprites,
    Dance and rouse the magic riot.

With my head upon your lap,
    Hold me close and never wake me.
Sing me dead and kiss me dead;
    Heart and soul and body – take me!

Eingehüllt in graue Wolken

Wrapped in clouds, as in a mantle,
    Now the great gods sleep together,
And I hear them bravely snoring,
    And we're having awful weather.

THE HOME-COMING

~~~~~~~~~~~~~~~~

It grows wilder; winds are howling,
    And the masts are bent like willows.
Who can curb the lordly tempest?
    Put a bridle on the billows?

I can't stop it, let it come then;
    Storms and terrors without number.
I will wrap my mantle round me,
    And, like any god, I'll slumber.

Der Wind zieht seine Hosen an

The wind pulls up his water-spouts,
    His white and foaming breeches;
He whips the waves; he storms and shouts.
    The whole sea heaves and pitches!

From the black skies, a furious might
    Impels the rain's commotion;
It seems as though primeval night
    Had come to drown the ocean.

To the mast a vagrant sea-gull clings
    With a hoarse shrilling and crying.
As though in despair she flaps her wings,
    An evil prophesying.

THE HOME-COMING

Der Sturm spielt auf zum Tanze

The storm tunes up for dancing,
    It yells and shrieks away.
Huzzah, how the old ship waltzes!
    The night is wild and gay.

A riot of tossing mountains,
    So seems the sea tonight.
Here, yawns a sinking chasm;
    There, looms a wall of white.

The sound of prayers and puking
    And oaths from the cabin come;
I cling to the mast with a vengeance,
    And wish that I were home!

Der Abend kommt gezogen

Over the sea's vast acres
    The misty night lay warm;
Secretly, from the breakers
    A white spray grew into form.

Out of the waves a mermaid
    Came without beckon or call;
We sat, and some inner stir made
    Her white breasts heave and fall.

She clasped me and caressed me;
More anguish than delight.
"Too closely hast thou pressed me,
O lovely water-sprite."

"Though my embrace is stormy
I am not rude nor bold;
It's you who must hold and warm me,
For the night is far too cold."

"The moon has reached its nadir;
Low clouds conceal its light.
Thine eyes grow wetter and sadder,
O lovely water-sprite."

"Grieve not for Neptune's daughter;
My eyes are sad and wet,
For I came from depths of water
And the salt is in them yet."

"I hear mad waters sounding;
I see the gulls take flight;
I feel thy wild heart pounding,
O lovely water-sprite."

"Truly, my heart is pounding,
Pounding, alas, too wild!
I love thee past telling or sounding,
Too dear, too mortal child."

THE HOME-COMING

Wenn ich an deinem Hause

I pass your little dwelling
    Each morning that is fair;
And I am thrilled, my darling,
    Whenever I see you there.

Your deep brown eyes disturb me,
    They question and condole;
"Who art thou, and what ails thee,
    Oh, pale and wandering soul?"

I am a German poet,
    In German lands I shine;
And where great names are mentioned
    They're bound to mention mine.

As for my sickness, darling,
    It's rather a common sign;
And where great griefs are mentioned
    They're bound to mention mine.

THE HOME-COMING
wwwwwwwwww

Das Meer erglänzte weit hinaus

The vastness of the ocean shone
  In the sunset's final gleaming.
We sat in the fisher's hut alone,
  Silent and secretly dreaming.

The mist crept up, the waters hove,
  The gulls kept coming and going;
And from her eyes that welled with love
  The quiet tears were flowing.

I saw them fall upon her hand,
  And then, as quickly sinking
Upon my knees, from that white hand
  I drank the tears, unthinking.

And from that hour my life has turned,
  And sorrow leaves me never.
That wretched woman's tears have burned
  And poisoned me forever.

Da droben auf jenem Berge

High up on yonder mountain
  A castle stands, and three
Fair maidens live within it;
  They love me generously.

99

Saturday, Yetta kissed me;
　　Sunday, Julia was free;
On Monday, Kunigunda
　　With love near smothered me.

But Tuesday, my three fair charmers
　　Gave an imposing fête;
The neighborhood's lords and ladies
　　Came riding in wagons of state.

But me they had skipped or forgotten,
　　And that was a mean thing to do.
Those gossips, the old aunts and cousins,
　　They noticed, and laughed at it, too.

Die Lilie meiner Liebe

My sweetheart has a lily
　　That dreams by a brook all day,
It turns from me, and stilly
　　Its beauty seems to say:

"Go, faithless man, your rapture
　　Has left me cold. Depart!
I saw you bend and capture
　　The rose with your fickle art."

THE HOME-COMING

Am fernen Horizonte

Wrapped in the distant sunset,
   Like phantoms in a mist,
I see the town and its towers,
   All rose and amethyst.

A damp sea-breeze is rising;
   The sea grows rough and dark.
With slow and sad precision
   The boatman rows my bark.

The sun looks up a moment
   Piercing the clouds above,
And shows me, all too clearly,
   The place I lost my love.

Sei mir gegrüsst, du grosse

Greetings to you, great city
   Of power and mystery,
That once, within your bosom,
   Shielded my love for me.

Tell me, O gates and towers,
   Where is my loved one, where?
Into your care I gave her;
   You should have kept her there.

THE HOME-COMING

I do not blame the towers,
  They could not stir where they stood,
When she, with her trunks and boxes,
  Stole off as fast as she could.

The gates, those fools, *they* let her
  Pass through them – and were still.
Well, fools are always willing
  When foolish women will.

So wandl' ich wieder den alten Weg

To old paths and familiar streets
  My footsteps have reverted;
And lo, there stands the belovèd's house,
  Desolate and deserted.

How close and narrow the streets have grown;
  The pavement itself is unstable!
The houses topple and seem to fall.
  I'm off as fast as I'm able!

  Ich trat in jene Hallen

I stood as in a spell
  Where she swore faith undying;
And where her tears once fell
  Serpents were hissing and lying.

THE HOME-COMING

Still ist die Nacht, es ruhen die Gassen

The night is still; the streets are quiet;
   My sweetheart dwelt in this house of yore.
Long since she left the city's riot;
   The house still stands as it stood before.

Here, too, there stands a man who gazes
   On heaven and wrings his hands in despair.
But when his face the moonlight glazes –
   It is myself that is standing there.

THE HOME-COMING

Oh, pale, worn shadow, oh, phantom double,
    Why ape my bitter, love-sick tears,
That drove me here to an endless trouble,
    Many a night in the vanished years?

Wie kannst du ruhig schlafen

How can you sleep so soundly,
    Knowing I'm living. See,
When the old rage comes on me,
    What is a yoke to me!

There is a song that tells how
    A lover dead and brave
Came to his lass at midnight,
    And brought her to his grave.

Believe me, child of beauty,
    Bright as the fiercest star,
I live, and am ten times stronger
    Than all the dead men are!

Die Jungfrau schläft in der Kammer

A maiden lies in her chamber
    Lit by a trembling moon;
Outside there rises and echoes
    A waltz's giddy tune.

THE HOME-COMING

ᴡᴡᴡᴡᴡᴡᴡᴡᴡ

"I wonder who breaks my slumber;
    I'll go to the window and see – "
And lo, a skeleton stands there;
    It fiddles and sings with glee:

"A dance you swore to give me,
    And you have broken your vow;
Tonight there's a ball in the churchyard;
    Come out and dance with me now!"

The maid, as though moved by magic,
    Obeys, and she leaves the house;
The skeleton, fiddling and singing,
    Goes on with its wild carouse.

It fiddles and leaps and dances
    And rattles its bones to the tune;
Its skull keeps nodding and nodding
    Crazily under the moon.

Ich stand in dunkeln Träumen

I stood bewildered, seeing
    Her picture there – and lo,
That fair, belovèd likeness
    Began to live and glow.

THE HOME-COMING

About her lips there trembled
   A laughter, strange and dear;
And, through the tears of sorrow,
   Her gleaming eyes shone clear.

Wet were my cheeks; the tear-drops
   Were falling fast and free...
And oh, I cannot believe it,
   That you are lost to me!

Ich unglücksel'ger Atlas! Eine Welt

I, unfortunate Atlas! A whole world,
A monstrous world of sorrows I must carry.
I bear a weight unbearable; a burden
That breaks the heart within me.

Oh, foolish heart, you have what you desired!
You would be happy, infinitely happy,
Or infinitely wretched, foolish heart.
And now – now you are wretched.

Die Jahre kommen und gehen

The years keep coming and going,
   Men will arise and depart;
Only one thing is immortal:
   The love that is in my heart.

THE HOME-COMING
〜〜〜〜〜〜〜〜〜〜

Oh, once, only once, might I see thee,
　　Ere I break these fetters in shards,
And kneel to thee, dying, and murmur:
　　"Madam, my best regards."

Mir träumte: Traurig schaute der Mond

I dreamed: The moon shone sadly down,
　　Sadly the stars were grieving;
They led me to the distant town
　　Where my beloved was living.

They led me safely to her abode;
　　I kissed the stones of the stairway,
Pressing the very steps she trod
　　Where her skirts had trailed their fair way.

The night was long; the night was cold;
　　Cold were the stones on the landing;
The moon revealed her, aureoled,
　　Still at the window standing.

Was will die einsame Träne

Why does this lonely tear-drop
　　Disturb my eyes again?
It lingers, a last reminder
　　Of days too distant for pain.

THE HOME-COMING

Once it had shining sisters;
    But, with the old delights
And passing griefs, they left me,
    Lost in the windy nights.

Lost, like the mist, those blue orbs,
    Stars with a smiling dart,
That shot the joys and sorrows
    Laughing into my heart.

Even my love has perished,
    A breath that I have drawn.
Oh, lone, belated tear-drop,
    'Tis time you, too, were gone.

Der bleiche, herbstliche Halbmond

The pale, autumnal half-moon
    Breaks through the cloudy skies;
Quietly by the churchyard
    The lonely parsonage lies.

The mother reads in her Bible;
    The son just stares and stares;
The elder daughter dozes;
    The younger one declares:

THE HOME-COMING

"Oh, Lord, how stupid the days are,
    Endlessly dull and drear!
Only when there's a funeral
    Is there anything doing here."

"You're wrong," says the mother still reading,
    "They've only buried four;
That is, since they laid your father
    There, by the churchyard door."

"Well," yawns the elder daughter,
    "I'll starve no longer with you.
I'll go to the Count tomorrow;
    He's rich, and he loves me, too."

The son then bursts out laughing,
    "At the 'Star' there are hunters three;
They're making gold, and gladly
    They'll teach the secret to me."

The mother flings her Bible
    At his head, half-crazed with grief,
"That's what you'll be, God help you,
    A common gutter-thief!"

Lo, there's a tap at the window;
    They turn to a beckoning hand.
There, in his moldy cassock,
    They see the dead father stand.

THE HOME-COMING

Das ist ein schlechtes Wetter

Well, this is awful weather,
  Storming with rain and snow.
I sit at the window staring
  Into the darkness below.

A little glimmering brightness
  Goes down the uncertain street:
A lantern, and a mother
  With tired and stumbling feet.

I think it's eggs and flour
  That the old lady has bought
To bake a cake for her daughter,
  The lazy good-for-naught.

Yawning at home on the sofa
  She lies in front of the blaze –
The golden hair is falling
  Around her golden face.

Man glaubt, dass ich mich gräme

They think that I am tortured
  Beneath a bitter yoke;
And I have come to believe it
  As well as other folk.

THE HOME-COMING

Child with big eyes, I've said it
   Too often, still it's true:
I love you beyond all telling,
   And love tears the heart in two.

But in my own room only
   I've said this thing – for see,
When I am in your presence
   No word escapes from me.

Heartless, inhuman angels
   Have sealed my lips somehow;
And through those evil angels
   I am in misery now.

Deine weissen Lilienfinger

Oh, your slim, white lily-fingers,
Only once more might I kiss them;
And, as to my heart I press them,
Lose myself in quiet weeping.

Your clear, violet-eyes pursue me;
Dance before me, day and night.
And I wonder how to answer,
How to solve those sweet, blue riddles.

THE HOME-COMING

"Hat sie sich denn nie geäussert"

"Has she never even shown you
    That your hot avowals moved her?
Did her dark eyes tell you nothing,
    When you swore how much you loved her?

"Could you never find an entrance
    To her soul through sighs and glances?
And they say you're not a donkey,
    But a hero of romances!"

Sie liebten sich beide, doch keiner

They loved one another, though neither
    Would speak to the other thereof;
They looked at each other like strangers
    The while they were dying of love.

They parted; and only in visions
    They met, and the dream soon fled.
And at last these two were buried –
    They scarcely knew they were dead.

THE HOME-COMING

Und als ich euch meine Schmerzen geklagt

When I told of my sorrows that wounded and tore
You answered with yawns and nothing more.
But now, since I've added a lyrical phrase
And put them in verse, you are lavish with praise!

Ich rief den Teufel und er kam

I called the devil and he came;
And then I saw, with a wondering gaze,
He was not hideous, he was not lame,
But a genial man with charming ways.
A man in the very flush of his prime;
Experienced, suave, and in touch with his time.
As a diplomat, his talent is great,
And he speaks wisely of Church and the State.

True, he is pale; but it's little wonder,
For Sanskrit and Hegel he's staggering under.
His favorite poet is still Fouqué;
As critic he finds that work is a bother,
So Hecaté now, his beloved grandmother,
Has taken the task and enjoys it, they say.
My legal studies called forth his laudation;
He, too, in his youth, found them quaint recreation.
He said that my friendship could never be
Too dear for him, and bowed to me,
And asked had we not met some place –
Perhaps the ambassador's? And with that sentence
I looked more closely at his face,
And recognized an old acquaintance.

Mensch, verspotte nicht den Teufel

Mortal, mock not at the devil;
   Life is short and soon will fail,
And the fire everlasting
   Is no idle fairy-tale.

Mortal, pay your debts, delay not.
   Years are long; and while they last
You will borrow in the future
   Just as much as in the past.

THE HOME-COMING

Die heil'gen drei Kön'ge aus Morgenland

Three holy kings from the Orient
    Asked in each town with wonder:
"What is the way to Bethlehem,
    And does the road lie yonder?"

But neither the young nor the old could tell;
    The three kings went on blindly.
They followed the lure of a golden star
    Whose light was brilliant but kindly.

The star stood still over Joseph's house;
    They entered with shining faces.
The oxen bellowed, the baby cried,
    And three holy kings sang praises.

Mein Kind, wir waren Kinder

My child, we once were children,
    Two children, blithe and gay,
We used to crawl up to the hen-house
    And hide ourselves under the hay.

We cackled and crowed whenever
    People passed down the road –
"Kikerikee!" They thought it
    Was really the cocks that crowed.

THE HOME-COMING

The boxes in our courtyard
    We draped with what we could find,
And lived in them together,
    A home of the coziest kind.

Our neighbor's cat came often
    To visit us in our bower;
We met her with bows and curtsies
    And compliments by the hour.

Politely we asked how her health was,
    In the course of a friendly chat.
(Since then we've said the same thing
    To many a grave, old cat.)

And often like old folk we gossiped,
    Aping their serious ways;
Complaining how things were better
    In the vanished "dear old days."

How Love and Faith and Honor
    Were lost without regret;
How coffee was so expensive,
    And money so hard to get!

Gone are the plays of childhood,
    And all things seem a wraith —
Time and the world and money,
    And Love and Honor and Faith.

THE HOME-COMING

~~~~~~~~~~~~~~~~

Das Herz ist mir bedrückt, und sehnlich

My heart is crushed with grief, for sadly
    I think of old times, clean of strife,
When all the world went far from badly,
    And people lived a normal life.

But now the world seems madly driven;
    Scrambling to pull and push ahead!
Dead is the good Lord up in Heaven,
    And down below the devil's dead.

All things, with this eternal shoving,
    Become a cheap and sodden brawl;
And if it were not for a little loving
    There'd be no rest for us at all.

Wie der Mond sich leuchtend dränget

As the moon through heavy cloud-drifts
    Bursts with his effulgent rays,
So a shining memory rises
    From the old and darkened days:

On the deck we sat, and drifted
    Down the Rhine as on a throne;
And the banks, bright green with summer,
    In the radiant twilight shone.

And there was a gracious lady;
  At her feet I sat and dreamed.
On that pale, dear face the ruddy,
  Burnished gold of sunset gleamed.

Lutes were ringing, boys were singing;
  Happiness on every side!
And the vault of Heaven grew bluer,
  And the very soul grew wide.

And there passed, as in a legend,
  Cliff and castle, wood and field.
And I saw them through her beauty;
  In her eyes they lay revealed.

Im Traum sah ich die Geliebte

I saw in a dream the belovèd,
  A woman careworn and gray,
The radiant, blossoming body
  Withered and fallen away.

One child in her arms she carried,
  And one by her hand was led;
And struggle and sorrow were written
  In her look, her clothes, her tread.

She stumbled toward the market,
　　And there she looked at me,
　And there I waited, saying
　　Calmly and mournfully:

"Oh, come with me to my dwelling,
　　For thou art sick and pale;
　And meat and drink I'll work for
　　To make thee whole and hale.

"And I will tend and cherish
　　Thy children undefiled;
　But thee, before all others,
　　Thou poor, unfortunate child.

"And I will never speak of
　　My love so torn and deep.
　And when at last thou diest,
　　Upon thy grave I'll weep."

Teurer Freund! Was soll es nützen

"Why, my friend, this same old fretting,
　　In the same, monotonous fashion?
　Will you be forever setting
　　On the addled eggs of passion?"

THE HOME-COMING

"Ah! It's no small task to tackle!
    First the chicks come, thin and sickly;
Then, when they begin to cackle,
    In a book you clap them, quickly."

Werdet nur nicht ungeduldig

Listen, do not grow impatient,
    Though I keep the old note ringing,
And you hear the old heart-sickness,
    Even in my latest singing.

Only wait – these dying echoes
    Soon will cease; and with new power,
Lo, a new, poetic springtime
    In a heart that's healed will flower.

Nun ist es Zeit, dass ich mit Verstand

Now it is time that I should start
    And leave all folly behind me.
As comic actor I've played my part
    In a comedy that was assigned me.

The settings were painted brilliant and bold
    In the latest romantic fashion;
My knightly mantle was splendid with gold;
    I thrilled with the noblest passion.

And now at last I must say good-bye
   To speeches once distracting.
But I am wretched, and I sigh
   As though I still were acting.

O God! unknown I spoke in jest
   The things I felt most deeply;
I've acted, with death in my very breast,
   The dying hero, cheaply.

Den König Wiswamitra

The good king Wiswamitra
   Has little quiet now;
He'll fight, he'll fret, he'll famish
   To get Wasishta's cow.

Oh, good king Wiswamitra,
   Oh, what an ox art thou;
Such penance and such passion –
   And all for just one cow!

Herz, mein Herz, sei nicht beklommen

Heart, my heart, let naught o'ercome you;
   Bear your destiny and pain.
   Spring will bring you back again
What the winter's taken from you.

THE HOME-COMING

And how much is left! The small things
  And the whole of earth is fair!
  Heart, you never need despair;
You can love, not one, but all things!

Du bist wie eine Blume

Child, you are like a flower,
  So sweet and pure and fair;
I look at you, and sadness
  Touches me with a prayer.

I lay my hands on your forehead
  And pray God to be sure
To keep you forever and always
  So sweet and fair – and pure.

Kind! Es wäre dein Verderben

Child, I know 'twould be your ruin,
  And my thoughts keep guard and turn there,
That your heart may not be kindled
  With the love that used to burn there.

But my too successful triumph
  Somehow does not quite delight me.
And I keep on thinking, hoping
  You might love me yet – despite me.

THE HOME-COMING

ᴡᴡᴡᴡᴡᴡᴡᴡᴡᴡ

Wenn ich auf dem Lager liege

When I lie down for comfort
  Upon the pillows of night,
There rises and floats before me
  A phantom clothed in light.

As soon as smiling slumber
  With soft hands locks my eyes,
Into my dream the vision
  Creeps with a sweet surprise.

But even with the morning
  The dream persists and stays;
The sunlight cannot melt it —
  I carry it through the days.

Mädchen mit dem roten Mündchen

Girl, whose mouth is red and laughing;
  Girl, whose eyes are soft and bright,
All my being moves about you,
  Thinking of you day and night.

Long, how long, this winter evening;
  And I yearn the whole night through
To be sitting, talking lightly,
  In the little room with you.

THE HOME-COMING

To my lips I would be pressing,
    Love, your slender, tender hand;
And my tears would tremble, blessing
    That belovèd and blessèd hand.

Mag da draussen Schnee sich türmen

Snows and storms may whirl in torrents;
And I watch, without abhorrence,
Hailstones at my windows storming;
For they never seem alarming
While my heart can hold this grace:
Spring – and one dear, Spring-like face.

THE HOME-COMING

Andre beten zur Madonna

Mary's praise is never done;
　　Others pray to Paul and Peter;
　　But my only prayer is sweeter,
For I worship thee, my sun.

Give me kisses, sweetly won,
　　Give my songs their shining cadence,
　　Loveliest sun among the maidens,
Loveliest maid beneath the sun!

Verriet mein blasses Angesicht

Did not my pallid face betray
　　The passion that I bore you?
And did you think my haughty lips
　　Would, beggar-like, implore you?

These haughty lips were only made
　　For kisses, jests, and lying –
They'd form a mocking, scornful word
　　Even though I were dying.

THE HOME-COMING

"Teurer Freund, du bist verliebt"

"Ah, my friend, you are in love,
    And new torments chain you tighter;
For your brain is growing duller
    As your foolish heart grows lighter.

"Yes, my friend, you are in love,
    Though the truth is unconfessed;
Why, I see your heart's blood glowing,
    Blushing, even through your vest!"

Ich wollte bei dir weilen

I sought your side, the only
    Peace that I ever knew;
You left me, worn and lonely.
    You had so much to do.

I said I gave you wholly
    Body and soul; and how
You laughed, laughed long and drolly,
    And made a twinkling bow.

With all these things you tried me;
    You even dared do this:
You roused me, then denied me
    The usual parting kiss.

THE HOME-COMING

Think not because of my snarling
   I'll shoot myself at your door!
All this, my precious darling,
   Has happened to me before.

Saphire sind die Augen dein

Sapphires are those eyes of yours,
   None lovelier or braver;
Thrice happy is the lucky man
   On whom they shine with favor.

Your heart is a warm diamond,
   A light that never dwindles.
Thrice happy is the lucky man
   For whom that fire kindles.

Twin rubies are those lips of yours,
   A rich and radiant measure.
Thrice happy is the lucky man
   Who can possess this treasure.

Oh, could I know that lucky man,
   And find that happy lover,
Nicely alone in some deep wood,
   His luck would soon be over.

THE HOME-COMING

Habe mich mit Liebesreden

I have lied to win you, precious;
    Now my breast against yours burns.
And I lie in my own meshes,
    And the jest to earnest turns.

And if ever you should leave me,
    With a jest, as is your right,
Earnestly, while fiends receive me,
    I will shoot myself that night.

Zu fragmentarisch ist Welt und Leben

Life in this world is a muddled existence –
Our German professor will give me assistance.
He knows how to whip the whole thing into order;
He'll make a neat System and keep it in line.
With scraps from his nightcap and dressing-gown's border
He'd fill all the gaps in Creation's design.

Ich hab' mir lang den Kopf zerbrochen

My head and brain are almost broken
    With dreams and thinking, night and day,
But now your eyes have solved the problem;
    They sweep my hesitance away.

THE HOME-COMING

And I will come to you quite boldly,
  And meet your eyes' sweet, silent call.
And once again I am a lover –
  Something I cannot grasp at all.

Sie haben heut' Abend Gesellschaft

They're having a party this evening
  And the house is gay with light.
Above, at a brilliant window,
  A shadow trembles in sight.

You see me not; in darkness
  I move alone, apart.
How little can you see, then,
  Into my darkened heart.

My darkened heart still loves you,
  Loves you and tortures me,
And breaks and lies here bleeding –
  But you will never see.

Ich wollt' meine Schmerzen ergössen sich

Oh, could I capture my sadness
  And pour it all into one word;
The glad-hearted breezes would lift it
  And carry it off, like a bird.

They'd bear it to you, oh, belovèd,
  That word of passionate care;
And every hour you'd hear it;
  'Twould follow you everywhere.

When you have scarce closed your eyelids,
  And slumber over them streams,
That word will arise and pursue you,
  Even into your dreams.

Du hast Diamanten und Perlen

You've pearls and you've diamonds, my dearest,
  You've all that most mortals revere;
And, oh, your blue eyes are the fairest —
  What else could you ask for, my dear?

Upon those blue eyes, my dearest,
  I've written for many a year
A host of immortal poems —
  What else could you ask for, my dear?

And with those blue eyes, my dearest,
  You wrought a bright torture here,
And lightly you led me to ruin —
  What else could you ask for, my dear?

THE HOME-COMING

Wer zum erstenmale liebt

He who, for the first time, loves,
Even vainly, is a god;
But the man who loves again,
And still vainly, is a fool.

Such a fool am I; the second
Time I love, still unrequited.
Sun and moon and stars are laughing;
And I laugh with them – and perish.

Zu der Lauheit und der Flauheit

In your tepid soul and vapid,
   There's no strength to stand the shocks
Of my wild love, with its rapid
   Force that breaks a path through rocks.

You, you want love's broad, safe high-roads,
   And a husband's arm through life;
Scorning all the glades and by-roads,
   Just a prim and pregnant wife.

THE HOME-COMING

~~~~~~~~~~~~~~~~

O, mein gnädiges Fräulein, erlaubt

Oh, loveliest of ladies, may
    This pale son of the Muses,
Upon thy swan-like bosom lay
    His head with Love's own bruises.

"Oh, sir! To say such things to me
Out loud – in front of company."

Gaben mir Rat und gute Lehren

Of words and advice they were the donors;
They even promised me lavish honors.
My future was rosy, my fame would be great;
They'd be my patrons – I need only wait.

But still, with all their patronization,
I would have died of slow starvation,
Except for a man who chanced to be made
Of splendid stuff and who came to my aid.

Excellent fellow! I look on and let him
Work for my dinner; I'll never forget him!
Ah, it's a pity that I never can
Kiss him – for I am that worthy man.

THE HOME-COMING

Diesen liebenswürd'gen Jüngling

This most amiable youngster
    Can't be spoken of too highly,
For with wines, liqueurs, and oysters
    He regales me, almost shyly.

Charming are his coat and trousers,
    And his ties are most appealing,
And he comes here every morning
    Just to ask how I am feeling.

Of my wide renown he gushes,
    Of my grace, my wit and humor;
And he swears to serve and help me,
    Grieving that he cannot do more.

And at many an evening party
  'Mid the ladies' panegyrics,
With inspired voice and features
  He recites my deathless lyrics.

Oh, to find so rare a fellow
  Makes me see the whole world gaily;
In these sorry times, above all,
  When his betters vanish daily.

Mir träumt: Ich bin der liebe Gott

I dreamt I was the dear Lord God
  And sat in Heaven proudly;
The angels clustered at my feet
  And praised my poems loudly.

Rich food I ate and sweetmeats, too,
  My costly taste displaying.
I washed them down with rare old wines,
  Without a thought of paying.

But the inaction bored me so,
  I longed once more to revel;
I thought, were I not God Himself,
  I'd rather be the devil.

THE HOME-COMING

"Ho, long-legged Gabriel," I called,
    "Put on thy boots, I prithee;
Seek out my good old friend, Eugene,
    And fetch him quickly with thee.

"Seek him not at the college halls,
    Seek him where wine inspires;
Seek him not at St. Hedwig's Church—
    Seek him at Ma'm'selle Meyer's.

The angel spread his plumes and flew
    Swift as a wingèd stallion,
And found and carried up to me
    My friend, the old rapscallion.

"See, lad, I am the Lord Himself,
    I rule each great and dumb thing;
I always told you some fine day
    I would amount to something.

"Here I work wonders every hour;
    Things that would quite enthuse you.
Today, for instance, I will change
    All Berlin, to amuse you.

"The cobble-stones in every street
    Shall split, and in each moister,
New-opened center shall be found,
    Juicy and fresh—an oyster.

"A rain of gentle lemon-juice
  Shall fall on them, bestowing
A grace; and lo, through all the streets,
  Rhine-wine shall keep on flowing.

"See how the folk of Berlin run;
  Their joy's too great to utter.
The heads of all the City Courts
  Are drinking from the gutter.

"And look how glad the poets are,
  How hungrily they rally!
The ensigns and lieutenants, too,
  Lap up each street and alley.

"The soldiers are the cleverest,
  Their shrewdness they display there.
They know that miracles like this
  Don't happen every day there."

Von schönen Lippen fortgedrängt, getrieben

Torn from bright lips I loved; departing sadly
  From those warm eyes that held me in their heaven.
I would have stayed another day, and gladly,
  But then the coach came up, and I was driven.

Child, that is life! A constant cry and wailing;
   A constant parting, though your arms enfold me.
Keep me . . . But ah, no spell can be unfailing.
   Even your eyes were powerless to hold me.

Ich hab' euch im besten Juli verlassen

It was in July that I lost you;
   In December I found you again.
Your warmth had vanished; the ardor had cooled;
   The chill was sharp as a pain.

Once more we will part, and when I return
   You will neither be hot nor be cold.
And there at the side of the grave I will yearn
   With a heart that is barren and old.

Wir fuhren allein im Dunkeln

Alone in the darkened post-chaise
   We sat and rode through the night.
Closely together we nestled;
   With laughter the hours were light.

But, oh, my love, next morning –
   And how we stared to find,
Sitting between us, Cupid,
   The boy that seemed so blind!

THE HOME-COMING

Wie dunkle Träume stehen

Like a dark dream the houses
   Stretch in a ghastly row;
Wrapped in my heavy mantle
   I pass them, silent and slow.

The tower of the cathedral
   Rings with the midnight hour;
And now my sweetheart is waiting
   With all her charms in flower.

The moon's my friend and companion,
   He lights the ways that are dim;
And as I come to her dwelling
   Gladly I call to him:

"I thank you, good old comrade,
   Through you no path was furled;
And now, since I must leave you,
   Go light the rest of the world.

"And if you find a lover
   Heaving a lonely sigh,
Console him as you consoled me,
   My friend, in the days gone by."

THE HOME-COMING

Das weiss Gott wo sich die tolle

God knows where I'll find that silly
    Madcap of a girl again;
I have searched this endless city,
    Wet and cursing in the rain.

Inns I've ransacked, tap-rooms, taverns —
    Everywhere that she was not;
I have asked each surly waiter,
    And a shrug was all I got.

Then I see her at a window,
    And she giggles — beckons ... Well!
Who could guess she'd ever stop at
    Such an elegant hotel!

Hast du die Lippen mir wund geküsst

With kisses my lips were wounded by you,
    So kiss them well again;
And if by evening you are not through,
    You need not hurry then.

For you have still the whole, long night,
    Darling, to comfort me.
And what long kisses and what delight
    In such a night may be!

THE HOME-COMING

Und bist du erst mein ehlich Weib

And when you're once my wedded wife
   You'll be the gayest one, dear;
For then you'll live the happiest life,
   With nought but pleasure and fun, dear.

And if you should scold I will not curse;
   'Twill be a matter of course, dear.
But, ah, should you disdain my verse,
   I'll get me a divorce, dear.

Als sie mich umschlang mit zärtlichem Pressen

When I am wrapped in her tender embraces,
   My soul seeks the skies like a thing that is driven!
I let it ascend; and meanwhile no place is
   As sweet as her lips, where I drink draughts of Heaven.

In den Küssen, welche Lüge

Oh, what lies there are in kisses!
   And their guile so well prepared!
Sweet the snaring is; but this is
   Sweeter still, to be ensnared.

THE HOME-COMING

Though your protests overwhelm me,
　　Still I know what you'll allow.
Yet I'll swear by all you tell me;
　　I'll believe all you avow.

An deine schneeweisse Schulter

Upon your snow-white shoulder
　　My weary head's at rest,
And I can hear the longing
　　That stirs within your breast.

The blue Hussars come bugling,
　　Come riding past your door;
And tomorrow, my love, you'll leave me
　　And I shall see you no more.

But though you will leave me tomorrow,
　　Today you are wholly mine,
Today you shall bless me doubly;
　　Closer your arms shall twine.

Es blasen die blauen Husaren

The blue Hussars go bugling
   Out of the town and away;
I come to you now, my sweetheart,
   Bringing a rose bouquet.

That was a mad, wild uproar;
   Crowding in every part.
But there was a place for many,
   Even in your small heart.

THE HOME-COMING

~~~~~~~~~~~~~~~~

Habe auch in jungen Jahren

In my youth when love was yearning,
I was often sad, and burning
   Like a cord of wood.
Now the price of fuel's higher,
And the cost has quenched the fire,
   Ma foi! and that is good.

Think of this, my pretty darlings,
Cease your silly tears and quarrelings,
   Stupid griefs and harms.
You have life, that precious bubble;
So forget love's ancient trouble,
   Ma foi! within my arms.

Bist du wirklich mir so feindlich

Have you really grown to hate me?
   Is the dreaded change completed?
Then the world shall hear my grievance,
   Hear how badly I've been treated.

Oh, ungrateful lips, how could you
   Utter such a shameful story
Of the man whose kisses thrilled you
   In those days of perished glory?

THE HOME-COMING

Ach, die Augen sind es wieder

Ah, these eyes again which always
    Made my welcome seem completer;
And these are the lips which always
    Made my harsh life somehow sweeter.

And the voice is just as always,
    When its lightest whisper gladdened.
Only *I* am not as always;
    I am home, but changed and saddened.

Now I feel white arms about me
    Close and passionately twining—
Yet I lie upon this bosom
    Unresponsive and repining.

Himmlisch war's, wenn ich bezwang

'Tis a heavenly pleasure indeed,
    Curbing passion's wild excess;
And when I do not succeed
    'Tis a pleasure none the less.

THE HOME-COMING

〰〰〰〰〰〰〰

Blamier mich nicht, mein schönes Kind

Don't shame me, darling; keep your place;
In public turn your pretty face.
But when we're home, and just we two,
Why, then I'll make it up to you.

Ja, Freund, hier Unter den Linden

Yes, friend, here *Unter den Linden*
   Your heart will be made gay
By women who have sinned in
   The very nicest way.

They blossom brightly, and know it;
   Their silks light up the street.
"Gay flowers," said a poet,
   "On little wandering feet."

Ah, those lovely hats and plumes!
   Ah, those shawls with their bright checks!
Lovely cheeks with their red blooms!
   And the lovelier, swan-like necks!

THE HOME-COMING

Selten habt ihr mich verstanden

Hard to understand your gabble;
  And my thoughts you fail to reach.
Only when in filth we dabble
  Do we find a common speech.

Doch die Kastraten klagten

And still the eunuchs grumbled,
  Whene'er my voice arose;
They grumbled as they mumbled
  My songs were far too gross.

And, oh, how sweetly thrilling
  Their little voices were;
Their light and limpid trilling
  Made such a pretty stir.

They sang of love, the leaping
  Flood that engulfs the heart...
The ladies all were weeping
  At such a feast of art!

THE HOME-COMING

Auf den Wällen Salamancas

On the walls of Salamanca
  Where the very winds are fonder,
Slowly, with my lovely Donna,
  In the summer dusk we wander.

And my arm is bent about her
  Slender body, and it lingers
As I feel her haughty bosom
  Heave beneath my happy fingers.

But a vague and threatening whisper
  From the linden makes me gloomy;
And the millwheel's evil murmur
  Sends a dark foreboding through me.

"Ah, Señora, something tells me
  Nevermore we two shall wander
On the walls of Salamanca,
  Where the very winds are fonder."

Kaum sahen wir uns, und an Augen und Stimme

As soon as we met we were wrapt in each other,
  Your eyes and your voice showed you would not resist;
And had it not been for that dragon, your mother,
  There, in that instant, I think we'd have kissed.

THE HOME-COMING

Tomorrow, alas, I must leave the quaint city
　　And go the old way, as if bound by a spell.
And you will look down from your window in pity;
　　And I – I will wave back a friendly farewell.

Über die Berge steigt schon die Sonne

Over the mountains the sun throws his fire;
　　The bells of the lambs in the distance are low.
My love and my lamb, my own sun of desire,
　　Once more I must see you before I can go.

I gaze at her window, impatient and muffled –
　　"My child, fare thee well; I am parting from thee!"
In vain! Nothing moves, not a curtain is ruffled;
　　For still she lies sleeping and dreaming ... of me?

Zu Halle auf dem Markt

　　In Halle's market-place
　　There stand two mighty lions.
　　Observe their hollow boldness; see
　　How quickly men have tamed them.

　　In Halle's market-place
　　There stands a mighty giant.
　　He has a sword, but wields it not;
　　Some fear has petrified him.

THE HOME-COMING

~~~~~~~~~~~~~~~~~~~~

In Halle's market-place
There stands a great cathedral,
Where peasantry and bourgeoisie
Have plenty of room to pray in.

Schöne, wirtschaftliche Dame

Lovely and efficient lady,
　　House and farm are well endowed;
And your cellar's well appointed,
　　And your fields are all well plowed.

In your clean and shining garden
　　Weeds can never raise their heads;
And the straw, when threshing's over,
　　Will be used to stuff the beds.

But your heart and lips, fair lady,
　　Fallow lie, as hard as stone;
And the bed is but half useful
　　Where you lie, and sleep alone.

THE HOME-COMING

Nacht liegt auf den fremden Wegen

Night lies on the strange, dark roadways;
   Weary limbs and heart distress me ...
Ah, sweet moon, through you my load weighs
   Lighter, as your soft beams bless me.

Radiant moon, your gentle wonder
   Sends night's ancient terrors reeling;
All my fears are torn asunder,
   And the happy tears come healing.

Der Tod, das ist die kühle Nacht

Death, it is but the long, cool night,
   And Life's a dull and sultry day.
   It darkens; I grow drowsy;
I am weary of the light.

Over my bed a strange tree gleams;
   There a young nightingale is loud.
   He sings of love, love only ...
I hear it, even in dreams.

THE HOME-COMING

Dämmernd liegt der Sommerabend

Softly now the summer twilight
   Lies upon the woods and meadows;
   And a golden moon looks downward
With a comforting and shy light.

By the brook and in its islands
   Crickets chirp; the water murmurs;
   And the wanderer hears a plashing
And a breathing in the silence.

There, alone, unclad, unfrightened,
   See, a water-nymph is bathing.
   How those white limbs in the water
And the moon are doubly whitened!

THE HOME-COMING

"Sag, wo ist dein schönes Liebchen"

"Where now is your precious darling,
    That you sang about so sweetly,
When the magic, flaming torrent
    Fired and filled your heart completely?"

Ah, that fire is extinguished,
    And my heart no longer flashes;
And this book's an urn containing
    All my love – and all its ashes.

TALES AND IDYLS

〰〰〰〰〰〰〰〰〰〰

DONNA CLARA

In dem abendlichen Garten

In the evening-colored garden
Wanders the Alcalde's daughter;
Festive throbs of drums and trumpets
Rise and echo from the castle.

"Oh, I weary of the dances,
And the cloying, fatuous phrases
Of the knights, who, bowing deeply,
To the sun itself compare me.

"Everything seems dull and tiresome
  Since by moonlight I beheld him,
  Him, my hero, whose sweet lute-strings
  Draw me nightly to my window.

"How he stood! So slim and fiery!
  And his eyes were burning boldly
  From his pale and classic features –
  Looking like St. George, the valiant."

Thus mused lovely Donna Clara,
  Gazing at the ground beneath her;
  As she looked up – lo, the handsome
  Unknown knight stood there before her.

Clasping hands with trembling passion,
  Now they wander in the moonlight;
  Now the flattering breeze is friendly;
  Great, enchanted roses greet them.

Great, enchanted roses greet them,
  Redder than love's flaming heralds...
"Ah, but tell me, my belovèd,
  Why these deep and sudden blushes?"

"Gnats were stinging me, my dearest,
  And I hate these gnats in summer;
  Hate them, love, as though they might be
  Nasty Jews with long, hooked noses."

"Jews and gnats – let us forget them,"
  Says the knight, with soft persuasion . . .
  From the almond tree a thousand
  Flower-flakes of white are falling.

  Flower-flakes of white are falling,
  And their perfume spills about them.
"Ah, but tell me, my belovèd,
  Is your heart mine, and mine only?"

"Yes, I love but you, my dearest,
  And I swear it by the Saviour,
  Whom the Jews, God's curse upon them,
  Did betray and foully murder."

"Jews and Saviour – let's forget them,"
  Says the knight, with soft persuasion . . .
  Far off in the dreamy distance
  Lilies gleam, with light surrounded.

  Lilies gleam, with light surrounded,
  Gazing at the stars above them.
"Ah, but tell me, my belovèd,
  Have you not, perhaps, sworn falsely?"

"Nothing's false in me, my dearest;
  Just as in my breast there courses
  Not a drop of blood that's Moorish,
  Nor a taint of Jewish foulness."

"Jews and Moors – let us forget them,"
Says the knight, with soft persuasion . . .
And, into a grove of myrtle,
Guides the fair Alcalde's daughter.

With love's soft and supple meshes
He has secretly entrapped her.
Short their words, but long their kisses;
And their hearts are running over.

Like a melting, poignant bride-song,
Sings the nightingale, uplifted;
Like a thousand torchlight dancers
Leap the fireflies from the bushes.

In the grove the stillness deepens.
Naught is heard except the murmurs
Of the wise and nodding myrtle
And the breathing of the flowers.

But the shock of drums and trumpets
Breaks out wildly from the castle,
And it wakes the lovely Clara
From the arms of her belovèd.

"Hark! They call to me, my dearest.
But before we part, pray tell me
What, my love, your own dear name is
That you've hidden so long from me."

And the knight, with gentle laughter,
Presses kisses on her fingers,
On her lips and on her forehead;
And at last he turns and answers:

"I, Señora, your belovèd,
  Am the son of the respected,
  Erudite and noble Rabbi
  Israel of Saragossa."

THE PILGRIMAGE TO KEVLAAR

1

Am Fenster stand die Mutter

The mother stood at the window;
    The son lay on the bed.
"Will you not rise up, William,
    And see the throng?" she said.

"I am so sick, my mother,
    I cannot hear or see;
The thought of my dead Gretchen
    Is all that lives in me."

"Rise up, and then to Kevlaar
    With book and cross we'll go;
God's Mother, She will heal you
    And rid your heart of woe."

The churchly banners flutter,
    Louder the chanting grows;
From Köln, beside Rhine River,
    The long procession goes.

The mother joins the pilgrims,
    She leads her son in the line,
And they, too, swell the chorus:
    "Queen Mary, praise be Thine!"

2

Die Mutter Gottes zu Kevlaar

The Mother of God in Kevlaar
 Puts on Her finest cloak –
Today they will keep Her busy,
 The crowds of wretched folk.

For all the sick in Kevlaar
 Bring Her, as offerings meet,
Limbs made of cunning waxwork,
 Wax arms and waxen feet.

And whoso brings a wax arm,
 His arm is healed of its wound;
And whoso brings a wax foot,
 His foot grows strong and sound.

Oh, many have come to Kevlaar
 On crutches, who danced away;
And many whose fingers were palsied
 Can take up the fiddle and play.

The mother bought a wax light,
 And molded therefrom a heart;
"Take this to Mother Mary,
 And She will ease the smart."

And, sighing, he took the wax heart,
    And, sighing, he knelt and prayed;
The tears in his eyes were trembling,
    And tremblingly he said:

"Oh, Holiest of the Holy,
    Virgin, divinely fair,
Empress of all the Heavens,
    To Thee I bring my care.

"At Köln with my aging mother
    I live within the town
Blest with a hundred churches
    And chapels of renown.

"And near us lived my Gretchen
    Who now lies underground –
Mary, I bring Thee a wax heart,
    Heal Thou my heart's great wound.

"Cure Thou my long heart-sickness,
    And daily, rain or shine,
Fervently I will worship.
    'Queen Mary, praise be Thine!' "

3

Der kranke Sohn und die Mutter

The heartsick son and his mother
    Were sleeping in the gloom,
And the Mother of God came softly,
    And entered the little room.

She bent down over the lover,
    And one white hand was drawn
Over his heart so gently . . .
    And, smiling, She was gone.

In a dream the mother saw this,
    And would have seen still more,
But the dogs' loud baying awoke her;
    She stumbled to the floor.

And there, stretched out and quiet,
    He lay, for he was dead.
And on his cheeks the daybreak
    Shone with a sudden red.

She folded her hands and sat there,
    She did not rail or whine;
She murmured over and over,
    "Queen Mary, praise be Thine!"

PROLOG TO "THE HARZ JOURNEY"

Schwarze Röcke, seidne Strümpfe

Black dress-coats and silken stockings,
  Cuffs of snowy white – beshrew them!
Soft embraces, oily speeches!
  Ah, if but a heart beat through them!

If a storm could stir your shirt-fronts,
  Ruffle them in any fashion!
Oh, you kill me with your maudlin
  Bursts of imitation passion.

I will go and climb the mountains,
  Where the simple huts are standing,
Where the winds blow fresh and freely,
  And a chest may try expanding.

I will go and climb the mountains,
  Where the mighty pine-trees tower,
Where the birds and brooks are singing,
  And the heavens grow in power.

Fare ye well, ye polished Salons,
  Polished folk and polished chaffing –
I will climb the rugged mountains,
  And look down upon you, laughing.

MOUNTAIN IDYL

1

Auf dem Berge steht die Hütte

On the mountain stands a cabin,
    Wherein lives a mountaineer;
All the evergreens are rustling
    And the moon turns golden here.

In the cabin there's an armchair
    Curiously carved and high.
He who sits in it is lucky;
    And that lucky man am I.

On the footstool there's a maiden,
    In my lap her arms repose;
Eyes like two blue stars that sparkle,
    And her mouth's a crimson rose.

No, the mother does not see us,
    For she spins and spins away;
And the father plays the zither,
    Singing some forgotten lay.

And the maiden whispers softly,
    Softly, almost breathlessly;
While a host of weighty secrets
    Gravely she confides to me.

"But since Auntie died," she tells me,
 "We can never hope to go
To the picnic-grounds at Goslar;
 That's the loveliest place I know.

"On the mountains here, it's lonely;
 Colder far than down below;
And in winter we are almost
 Lost and buried in the snow.

"Though I'm quite a girl, I tremble
 Like a child that's seized with fright,
At the evil mountain spirits
 And the things they do by night."

Suddenly she stops, as though her
 Own words chill and terrorize;
And she raises both hands quickly,
 Quickly covering her eyes.

In the trees the rustling's louder,
 Faster still the wheel is stirred,
And above the tinkling zither
 Something of the song is heard:

"Do not fear, my child, my darling,
 Fear no spirit's evil might!
Overhead, my child, my darling,
 Angels guard thee day and night!"

2

Tannenbaum, mit grünen Fingern

Now the fir-tree's long, green fingers
    Tap against the window-pane,
And the moon, that quiet listener,
    Sheds a flood of golden rain.

Father, mother, sleeping soundly,
    Snore for hours without a break;
But we two, with lively chatter,
    Keep each other wide awake.

"That you spend much time in praying
    I've my doubts; for always there
Is a sneer about your features
    That was never taught by prayer.

"Oh, that sneer, so cold and cruel,
    Makes me shiver, though I know
You are kind. Your eyes are gentle,
    And they have a tender glow.

"Yet I doubt that you believe in
    The inspired faith of most.
Do you worship God the Father,
    And the Son and Holy Ghost?"

"Ah, my child, while still an infant,
   While at mother's knee I stood,
I believed in God the Father,
   He whose rule is great and good.

"He who made the earth we dwell on,
   And the people here below;
He who made sun, moon, and planets,
   Teaching them the way to go.

"Then, my child, as I grew older,
   My belief had but begun,
And I mastered many new things,
   And I worshiped God and Son;

"The Belovèd Son, who, loving,
   Gave us love to bless and guide;
And for his reward, as usual,
   Was condemned and crucified.

"Now that I've matured and learned much,
   Read and roamed from coast to coast,
Now my heart, with deep conviction,
   Bows before the Holy Ghost.

"He has worked the greatest wonders,
   And he works them still; he broke,
Once for all, the tyrant's power,
   And he burst the bondman's yoke.

"All the ancient scars have vanished,
    Justice takes its rightful place;
  Now all men are free and equal
    In a pure and noble race.

"Mists and every evil fancy
    That had filled each night and day,
  Cares that crowded out our gladness –
    These have all been swept away!

"And a thousand armored champions
    He has sanctified and sent
  To fulfill his sacred mission,
    Fired with their high intent.

"Lo, their splendid swords are shining
    And their tossing flags are bright! –
  What, my child, you long to look on
    Such a proud and holy knight?

"Well, my darling, come and kiss me;
    Look at me and you can boast
  You have known just such a doughty
    Champion of the Holy Ghost."

3

Still versteckt der Mond sich draussen

Still the bashful moon is hiding
　　Close behind the evergreen;
And the lamp upon the table
　　Flickers and is scarcely seen.

But those two blue stars are shining
　　O'er the heaven of her cheeks;
And the crimson rose is glowing,
　　And the lovely child still speaks.

"Tiny goblins, imp-like fairies,
　　Clean our little cupboard bare;
It is full of food at evening,
　　But at daylight – nothing's there!

"And the thieving Little People
　　Skim our cream, our very best;
Then they leave the pans uncovered
　　And the cat licks up the rest.

"And that cat's a witch, I know it;
　　For she slinks off every night
To the old and ruined castle
　　On the haunted mountain-height.

"Once a mighty castle stood there,
    Full of armor and romance;
Shining knights and lovely ladies
    Laughed in many a torchlight dance.

"Then an old enchantress cursed it,
    Cursed each stone and winding stair.
Now there's nothing left but ruins;
    And the owls are nesting there.

"But my dear old aunt once told me
    If one speaks the Word of Might
At the proper, magic moment,
    And the hour and place be right,

"Then the castle shall be lifted
    From the ruined stones – and then
All the vanished knights and ladies
    Will arise and dance again.

"And who speaks that Word of Magic,
    Knights and ladies, wall and tower,
All are his; while drums and trumpets
    Hail his new and happy power."

Thus the fairy legends blossom
    From her mouth, that rose-in-bloom,
While her eyes are pouring starlight
    In the still and darkened room.

Round my hands she winds her golden
    Tresses, binding me at will;
Gives my fingers pretty nicknames;
    Kisses, laughs – and then grows still.

And the hushed room edges closer,
    Watching with a friendly light...
Table, chest – it seems I must have
    Seen them all before tonight.

Amiably the old clock gossips,
    And the zither, scarcely heard,
Plays itself with airy fingers;
    And, as in a dream, I'm stirred.

This must be the proper hour;
    Yes, the time and place are right.
And I think I feel it gliding
    From my lips – that Word of Might.

Do you see, my child, how quickly
    Midnight trembles now and breaks!
Brooks and pine-trees murmur louder,
    And the ancient mountain wakes.

Clang of zither, elfin voices
    Rise from glens and fairy bowers,
And a wild, fantastic springtime
    Brings a forest full of flowers.

Flowers, trembling and audacious,
  Flowers, strangely broad and tall,
Fling their eager scents and colors
  As though passion swayed them all.

Roses, red as flame, and burning
  From the brilliant tumult, rise;
Lilies, like great crystal columns,
  Tower straight into the skies.

And the stars, with fiery longing,
  Great as suns, look down and blaze,
Till the lilies' hearts are flooded
  With those bold, transforming rays.

But ourselves, my child, are altered
  More than all of these – for see!
Gleaming torches, silks and jewels
  Shimmer 'round us radiantly!

You, you have become a princess,
  And this hut's a castle tall;
Knights and ladies dance rejoicing;
  And there's magic over all.

Ah, but *I* have won the castle,
  Knights and ladies, wall and tower;
Even you – as drums and trumpets
  Hail my new and happy power!

THE HERD-BOY

König ist der Hirtenknabe

He's a king, this happy herd-boy,
　And his throne's the grassy down,
While the sun above his forehead
　Is his great and golden crown.

At his feet the sheep are lying,
　Flattering courtiers, soft and sly;
And his cavaliers are cattle,
　Pompously parading by.

And the kids are his court-players,
　Birds that flute before they drowse
Make a rustic chamber-music
　With the gentle bells of cows.

And they ring and sing so sweetly,
    And the soothing murmurs creep
From the waterfall and forest,
    That the young king falls asleep.

Like a minister, his watch-dog,
    Governs with an open ear;
And his loud, suspicious barking
    Makes the very echoes fear.

Sleepily the young king murmurs:
    "Ah, to rule is hard and mean.
How I wish that I were home now
    With my cozy little queen!

"On her dear and queenly bosom
    Soft my regal head would lie;
And I'd find my ancient kingdom
    Shining in each love-lit eye."

ON THE BROCKEN

Heller wird es schon im Osten

Comes a spark, the sun's first glimmer;
    And the eastern sky's in motion.
Far and faint the mountain summits
    Float upon a misty ocean.

Had I seven-league boots, I'd hasten
　　With the wind, as fast as telling;
Running on the tops of mountains
　　Till I reach my dear one's dwelling.

I would draw the curtains softly
　　From her bed, where she lies dreaming;
Softly I would kiss her forehead
　　And her lips, twin rubies gleaming.

And still softer I would whisper
　　In her frail and lily ear, "Love,
Dream we've never lost each other,
　　Dream we're lovers still, my dear love."

ILSE

Ich bin die Prinzessin Ilse

I am the Princess Ilse
　　And I dwell at Ilsenstein.
Come with me to my castle,
　　Thou shalt be blest, and mine.

There I shall bathe thy forehead
　　With waters clear and glad,
Until thy pain shall vanish,
　　Thou sick and sorrowing lad.

With my white arms about thee,
    Upon my breast thou'lt be;
And thou shalt lie there dreaming
    Of fairy legendry.

And I shall kiss and hold thee
    As I would kiss and hold
My lover, dear King Heinrich,
    Who now lies dead and cold.

The dead stay dead forever,
    Only the living live,
My laughing heart is leaping;
    I've youth and joy to give.

Then come down to my castle,
    Come to my crystal halls;
The knights and maidens are dancing,
    Happy are all my thralls.

There's rustling of silk and clatter
    Of spurs, and the bright air hums;
The nimble dwarfs are playing
    On fiddles and horns and drums.

But always my arms shall enfold thee
    And I shall keep thee enthralled;
As I stopped the ears of King Heinrich
    When the brazen trumpets called.

FROM "THE NORTH SEA"

CORONATION

Ihr Lieder! Ihr meine guten Lieder!

Ye songs! Ye valiant songs of mine
Up, up, and arm yourselves!
Let all the trumpets echo,
And lift this blossoming girl
Upon my shield.
For now my restless heart
Longs for her rule, proclaims her Queen.

Hail to thee, hail, oh, youthful Queen!

From the fierce sun at noon
I'll tear the red and gleaming gold,
And it shall be a diadem
For thy belovèd head.

176

From the great, waving, blue silk tent of heaven,
Where all the diamonds of the night are flashing,
I'll cut a mighty piece;
And hang it, like a royal mantle,
About thy royal shoulders.
I'll give thee a kingly dower
Of starched and polished sonnets,
Haughty tercets, proud and courtly stanzas.
For Pages I shall give thee my wit;
For Court-fool, my wild imagination;
For Herald, with laughing tears in his escutcheon,
My Humor shall serve thee . . .
But I, myself, dear Queen,
I humbly kneel before thee,
And present to thee, from the velvet cushion,
With deepest homage,
The little reason
That mercifully has been left me
By thy predecessor in the realm.

TWILIGHT

Am blassen Meeresstrande

On the pale strip of seashore
I sat alone, lost among fugitive thoughts.
The sun was sinking lower and threw
Glowing, red beams upon the water.
And the white, widening line of waves,
Pulled by the urging tide,
Rolled in and rumbled nearer and nearer —
A curious mingling of wailing and whistling,
Of laughing and murmuring, sighing and shouting;
And, under it all, the strange croon of the ocean.
It was as though I heard forgotten stories,
Ancient and lovely legends,
That once I had heard as a child
From our neighbor's children,
When we, in the summer evening,
On the stone-steps before the door,
Huddled together and listened
With eager hearts,
And sharp, inquisitive eyes . . .
While the growing girls
Sat at the opposite windows;
Their heads showing above the fragrant flower-pots,
Faces like roses;
Laughing and moon-illumined.

NIGHT ON THE STRAND

Sternlos und kalt ist die Nacht

The night is starless and cold,
The ocean yawns.
And, flat on his belly, the monstrous North-wind
Sprawls upon the sea.
Wheezing and groaning,
He babbles his hoarse confidences,
Like a crotchety grumbler who has grown good-humored;
Babbles to the listening waters.
Wild tales he tells them,
Tales of giants, tales of furious slaughter,
And old-world stories out of Norway.
And, between times, he laughs and bellows
Incantations from the Eddas,
And oaths and runes
So potent and so darkly magical
That the white sea-children
Leap up turbulently,
In waves of exultation.
Meanwhile, on the flat shore,
Over the surf-dampened sands,
A stranger walks
With a heart that is wilder than winds or waters.
Wherever he tramps
Sparks fly and sea-shells crunch and crumble.

He wraps himself in his gray, gloomy mantle
And strides on quickly through the windy night –
Led safely by the little taper
That beckons and shimmers with promise
From the lonely fisherman's cottage.

Father and brother are out at sea,
And alone,
All alone in the cottage, she sits,
The fisher's lovely daughter.
She sits at the hearth
And listens to the kettle
Singing its droning, drowsy song.

And she shakes fuel and heaps sticks on the fire
And blows on it,
So that the flickering red light
Lights up, with a lovely magic,
That blossoming face,
Those soft white shoulders
That stand out strangely from the coarse, gray shirt;
Shines on those small and careful hands
That are binding the little petticoat
Tighter about her waist.

Suddenly the door springs open
And the nocturnal stranger enters.
Confident with love, his eyes are fixed
On the white, slender girl,
Who trembles before him,
Like a frail and frightened lily.
And he drops his mantle on the ground
And smiles and says:

"Behold, my child, I keep my word;
   I come – and with me come
   The ancient times, when all the gods
   Came down from Heaven to the daughters of men,
   And embraced them
   And begat with them
   Scepter-bearing races of kings,
   And heroes, shakers of the world . . .
   But, child, do not stand astonished any longer,

Amazed at my divinity;
But get me, I beg of you, some tea with rum,
For it's cold outside.
And on such raw nights
We shiver – even we, who are immortal.
And, being gods, we catch ungodly sneezings,
With colds and coughings that are almost deathless."

THE SEA HAS ITS PEARLS

Das Meer hat seine Perlen

The sea has its pearls,
The heaven its stars,
But my heart, my heart,
My heart has its love.

Great is the sea and the heaven,
But my heart is greater still;
And fairer than pearls or stars
Glistens and sparkles my love.

Oh, young and lovely maiden,
Come to my fathomless heart;
My soul, and the sea, and the heavens
Are wasting away with love.

NEW SPRING

~~~~~~~~~~~~~~~~~~~~

SONGS

Gekommen ist der Maie

Here's May again, with its lifting
  Of leaves and voices high;
And rosy clouds are drifting
  Across an azure sky.

A nightingale is singing
  In every bower and croft;
And little lambs are springing
  Where fields are clover-soft.

But I am not singing or springing;
  I lie on a grassy plot,
Hearing a distant ringing,
  And dreaming of God knows what.

NEW SPRING

Leise zieht durch mein Gemüt

Lightly swinging bells are ringing
  With a soft insistence;
Tinkle, tiny tunes of spring,
  Tinkle through the distance.

Fill the air and run to where
  All the flowers grow sweeter.
If you see a rosebud there
  Tell her that I greet her!

NEW SPRING

Der Schmetterling ist in die Rose verliebt

The butterfly is in love with the rose,
   And flutters about her all day,
While he, in turn, is pursued by a bright
   Sunbeam that follows his way.

But wait – with whom is the rose in love?
   For whom does she tremble and pale?
Is it the silent evening star?
   The passionate nightingale?

I do not know whom the red rose loves;
   But I love you all, for I
Sing nightingale, sunbeam, and evening star,
   The rose and the butterfly!

Es erklingen alle Bäume

All the trees are full of music;
   Nesting birds repeat the call.
In this green, orchestral concert,
   Who's conductor of it all?

Can it be that old, gray plover
   Who keeps nodding to the beat?
Or that pedant, who, up yonder,
   Marks his "Cuckoo" strong and sweet?

Or is it the stork, who gravely
   Keeps on tapping with his bill,
Just as though he were directing,
   While the others soar and trill?

No; my own heart holds the leader;
   Well he knows the stress thereof!
And I feel the time he's beating,
   And I think his name is love.

Im Anfang war die Nachtigall

"In the beginning was the word,
   Sung by the nightingale, '*Sweet! Sweet!*'
While grass and apple-blossoms stirred,
   And violets found their dancing feet.

"He bit his breast until the blood
   Ran freely, and from that bright stream
A tall and lovely rose-tree stood;
   And there he sings his passionate dream.

"All of us birds now live in peace;
   His blood redeemed all things that fly.
Yet if the rosy song should cease
   The wood, and all it holds, would die."

So, to his brood, the sparrow speaks,
    As though he had them all in church;
The mother-bird is proud, and squeaks
    Upon her ministerial perch.

She's a good housewife, every day
    She only lives to build and breed;
While he, to pass the time away,
    Lectures his children in the creed.

Es drängt die Not, es läuten die Glocken

I must go forth, the bells are pealing;
    And, oh, I've lost my head completely.
A pair of eyes, in league with springtime,
    Have been conspiring far too sweetly.

A pair of brilliant eyes and springtime
    Storm at my heart and have incensed me;
Even the nightingales and roses,
    I think, are in a plot against me.

NEW SPRING

Ach, ich sehne mich nach Tränen

Ah, I long for tears returning
    Love and all its tender pain;
And I fear that very yearning
    Soon will be fulfilled again.

Love, that unction never failing,
    Love, that torture self-revealed,
Steals once more into an ailing
    Bosom that is barely healed.

Die schlanke Wasserlilie

The slender water-lily
    Stares at the heavens above,
And sees the moon who gazes
    With the luminous eyes of love.

Blushing, she bends and lowers
    Her head in a shamed retreat —
And there is the poor, pale lover,
    Languishing at her feet!

NEW SPRING

~~~~~~~~~~~~~~~~

Was treibt dich umher in der Frühlingsnacht

What drives you out in this night of spring
To set the flowers murmuring?
   The violets are affrighted;
The roses, flushed with shame, are red;
The lilies, paler than the dead,
   Bend as though they were blighted.

Oh lovely moon, what second sight
Inspires the flowers, for they are right;
   My crime is not forgiven.
How could I know the flowers had heard
The frantic prayers and the absurd
   Vows I had made to Heaven!

Mit deinen blauen Augen

   Your eyes' blue depths are lifted,
     With love and friendship stirred.
   They smile; and, lost in dreaming,
     I cannot speak a word.

   Your eyes and their deep heavens
     Possess me and will not depart:
   A sea of blue thoughts rushing
     And pouring over my heart.

NEW SPRING

Ich wandle unter Blumen

I wander where budding bowers
    Infect me with romance;
My soul expands with the flowers,
    Dizzy, as though in a trance.

Hold me! or drunken with utter
    Joy at the spell you invoke,
Here at your feet I totter –
    And the garden is full of folk!

Sag mir wer einst die Uhren erfund

Come, tell me whose super-intelligent power
Invented the second, the minute, the hour.
It must have been someone afraid of delight
Who sat in his house through a long winter night
And counted the strokes of the mice pick-picking,
And the measured beat of the death-watch ticking.

And who do you think first invented the kiss?
A lover who laughed when he first tasted bliss.
He kissed with conviction that brooked no delay;
He kissed all through April, he kissed all through May;
He kissed till the thrushes were shamed into singing,
And the great, laughing sun set the whole world ringing.

Es war ein alter König

There was an agèd monarch;
    His heart and head were gray with strife,
This poor old monarch wedded
    A young and lovely wife.

There was a pretty page-boy;
    His hair was light, his heart was clean,
He carried the long and silken
    Train of the fair young queen.

You know the old, old story
    So sweet to hear, so sad to tell.
Both of them had to perish;
    They loved each other too well.

NEW SPRING

In meiner Erinn'rung erblühen

In memory many pictures
    Arise and reassemble –
What gives your voice the magic
    That makes me burn and tremble?

Oh, do not say you love me!
    All that may bloom most brightly,
Love and the fires of April,
    You put to shame so lightly.

Oh, do not say you love me!
    But kiss in quiet closes,
And laugh when, in the morning,
    I show you withered roses.

Morgens send' ich dir die Veilchen

Every morn I send you violets
    Which I found in woods at dawn;
And at evening I bring roses
    Which I plucked when day had gone.

Do you know what these two flowers
    Say, if you can read them right?
Through the day you shall be faithful,
    And shall turn to me at night.

NEW SPRING

Der Brief, den du geschrieben

Your letter does not move me
    Although the words are strong;
You say you will not love me –
    But ah, the letter's long.

Twelve pages, neat and double.
    A little essay! Why,
One never takes such trouble
    To write a mere good-bye.

Sterne mit den goldnen Füsschen

Stars with golden feet are walking
    Through the skies with footsteps light,
Lest they wake the earth below them,
    Sleeping in the lap of night.

All the silent forests listen;
    Every leaf's a small, green ear;
And the dreaming mountain stretches
    Shadowy arms that reach me here.

Hush, who called there? My heart trembles
    As the dying echoes fail.
Was it my beloved, or was it
    Just a lonely nightingale?

NEW SPRING

Die holden Wünsche blühen

The sweet desires blossom
    And fade, and revive, and spend
Their beauty and wither, and blossom –
    And so on, without end.

I know this, and it saddens
    My life and all its zest.
My heart's so wise and clever
    It bleeds away in my breast.

Spätherbstnebel, kalte Träume

Autumn mists, cold dreams are filling
    Height and valley, while the thinned
Trees, poor ghosts, give their unwilling
    Leaves to bait the brutal wind.

One tree there, and one tree only,
    Holds its leaves untouched by dread;
There, among the gaunt and lonely
    Crowd, it lifts a dauntless head.

The scene's my heart: the same grim capture
    Kills the dearest dreams we knew.
Yet where all is stripped and sapped, your
    Face appears. The tree is you.

A GARLAND OF GIRLS

〰〰〰〰〰〰〰〰〰〰〰〰

SERAPHINE

Wandl' ich in dem Wald des Abends

Through the dusky wood I wander,
　　Through the dream-invoking glade,
While your spirit is beside me
　　Like the shadow of a shade.

Is not that your white veil drifting?
　　This your softly shining face?
Or is merely moonlight sifting
　　Through dark fir-trees for a space?

And this sound of weeping, is it
　　My own sorrow that I hear?
Can it, somehow, be my loved one
　　Who has really shed a tear!

195

An dem stillen Meeresstrande

Night has come with silent footsteps,
 On the beaches by the ocean;
And the waves, with curious whispers,
 Ask the moon, "Have you a notion

"Who that man is? Is he foolish,
 Or with love is he demented?
For he seems so sad and cheerful,
 So cast down yet so contented."

And the moon, with shining laughter,
 Answers them, "If you must know it,
He is both in love *and* foolish;
 And, besides that, he's a poet!"

Wie neubegierig die Möwe

How this too anxious sea-gull
 Follows us even here,
Because your lips come closer
 And closer to my ear.

Need I confess I'm filled with
 More wonder than the bird's;
Anxious if I'm to be thrilled with
 Your kisses or your words.

If I were only certain
   What shakes my pulse like this!
Tauntingly intermingled
   Are promise and the kiss.

Schattenküsse, Schattenliebe

Shadow-love and shadow-kisses,
   Shadow-life – you think it strange?
Fool! Did you imagine this is
   Fixed and constant, free from change?

Everything we love and cherish
   Like a dream, goes hurrying past;
While the hearts forget and perish,
   And the eyes are closed at last.

Das Fräulein stand am Meere

Upon the shore, a maiden
 Sighs with a troubled frown;
She seems so sorrow-laden
 To see the sun go down.

Don't let the old thing grieve you,
 Look up and smile, my dear;
For, though in front he may leave you,
 He'll rise again in the rear.

Wie schändlich du gehandelt

I've told no man how shameful
  You were, and how malicious;
But I have sailed away to the sea
  And told it to the fishes.

Upon the land I've left your
  Good name, so none may doubt you.
But through the length and depth of the sea,
  Everyone knows about you!

ANGELIQUE

Wie rasch du auch vorüberschrittest

Although you hurried coldly past me,
  Your eyes looked backward and askance;
Your lips were curiously parted,
  Though stormy pride was in your glance.

Would I had never tried to hold you,
  Nor seek your white and flowing train.
Would I had never found your footsteps,
  Or seeking them, had sought in vain.

Now, all your pride and wildness vanished,
   You are as tame as one could be;
Gentle, and sweet beyond endurance –
   And, worse, you are in love with me!

Wie entwickeln sich doch schnelle

How from such a chance beginning
   And in what a casual fashion,
There has grown so close a union,
   Such a great and tender passion.

Every day this charming creature
   Holds me faster in her power,
And the feeling that I love her
   Grows upon me hour by hour.

And her soul is lovely? Frankly,
   That's a matter of opinion;
But I'm sure of all the other
   Charms she shows to me, her minion:

Those white lips and that white forehead.
   Nose that wrinkles on occasion,
When her lips curve into laughter –
   And how swift is their persuasion!

∿∿∿∿∿∿∿∿∿∿∿

Ach, wie schön bist du, wenn traulich

Ah, how sweet you are, confiding
    All your thoughts to me, your lover,
When, with noble words and phrases,
    Your impulsive mind runs over.

When you tell me that your thoughts are
    Large and of a lofty fashion;
How your heart's pride, not too stubborn,
    Is at war with your compassion.

How you'd never give yourself for
    Millions – no, you could not bear it!
Ere you sold yourself for money
    You would rather die, you swear it!

And I look at you and listen,
    And I listen till you've finished,
Like a thoughtful, silent statue
    Whose belief is undiminished.

Ich halte ihr die Augen zu

I close her eyes, and keep them tight
    Whene'er we come to kiss;
Her laughter, curious and bright,
    Asks me the cause of this.

From early morn till late at night
   She questions why it is
I close her eyes and keep them tight
   Whene'er we come to kiss.

I do not even know – not quite,
   What my own reason is.
I close her eyes, and keep them tight
   Whene'er we come to kiss.

Wenn ich, beseligt von schönen Küssen

When in your arms and in our kisses
   I find love's sweet and happiest season,
My Germany you must never mention –
   I cannot bear it: there is a reason.

Oh, silence your chatter on anything German;
   You must not plague me or ask me to share it.
Be still when you think of my home or my kindred –
   There is a reason: I cannot bear it.

The oaks are green, and the German women
   Have smiling eyes that know no treason;
They speak of Love and Faith and Honor.
   I cannot bear it: there is a reason.

A GARLAND OF GIRLS

∧∧∧∧∧∧∧∧∧∧∧∧∧∧∧

Fürchte nichts, geliebte Seele

Do not fear, my love; no danger
    Ever will approach us here;
Fear no thief or any stranger.
    See, I lock the door, my dear.

Do not fear the wind that's quarreling,
    For these walls are strong and stout;
To prevent a fire, my darling,
    See, I blow the candle out.

Let my arms fold close and thickly
    Here about your neck and all –
One can catch a cold so quickly
    In the absence of a shawl.

Während ich nach andrer Leute

While I seek forbidden pastures,
    While, to put it briefly, I
Underneath some stranger's window
    All night long parade and sigh,

Then, perhaps, some other lover
    Paces just as anxiously
Underneath the very window
    Where my sweetheart lives with me.

That is human. God in Heaven,
　　Who can tell what may befall
In this labyrinth of living!
　　So it goes. God keep us all.

Ja, freilich, du bist mein Ideal

Yes, surely, you are my ideal;
　　Your beauty makes me dizzy.
Have I not proved the fact with zeal?
　　But just today I'm busy.

Tomorrow between two and three,
　　Impatient little sinner,
Immoderate flame will quicken me –
　　And after, there'll be dinner.

Perhaps, if there is still a seat,
　　I'll take you, on the level,
To opera as a special treat;
　　They're playing *Robert the Devil*.

It is a very grand affair
　　Of spells and love unlawful;
The music is by Meyerbeer,
　　The text by Scribe – godawful!

Schaff mich nicht ab, wenn auch den Durst

Don't send me off, now that your thirst
　　Is quenched, and all seems stale to you;
Keep me a short three months or more,
　　Then I'll be sated, too.

If now you will not be my love
　　Then try to be my friend;
Friendship is something that may come
　　When love comes to an end.

HORTENSE

Wir standen an der Strasseneck'

We stood upon the corner, where,
　　For upwards of an hour,
We spoke with soulful tenderness
　　Of love's transcending power.

Our fervors grew; a hundred times
　　Impassioned oaths we made there.
We stood upon the corner – and,
　　Alas, my love, we stayed there!

The goddess Opportunity,
  A maid, alert and sprightly,
Came by, observed us standing there,
  And passed on, laughing lightly.

DIANE

Diese schönen Gliedermassen

Such magnificent expanse,
  Such long lines of bone and muscle
Should provoke inspired chants;
  They are, may I say, colossal.

Should I overcome them by
  Unforeseen romantic ruses,
I'd be sorry for it; I
  Would emerge a mass of bruises.

Goddess with a heavenly length,
    Bosom, throat, and neck enslave me;
Ere I love you, give me strength,
    But should *you* embrace, God save me!

Steht ein Baum im schönen Garten

SHE SPEAKS:

Deep within a lovely garden
    There's an apple on a tree;
And, about the boughs, a serpent
    Coils itself and looks at me.
I can't take my eyes from off it,
    While I hear its gentle hiss,
For its eyes burn with a promise
    And a prophecy of bliss.

THE OTHER SPEAKS:

'Tis the fruit of life you see there,
    Taste it, do not let it fall;
Lest you throw away a lifetime
    Without knowing life at all.
Come, my darling, my sweet pigeon,
    Try it, taste it, do not fear;
Follow my advice and thank me.
    Trust your wise old aunt, my dear.

CLARISSA

Geh nicht durch die böse Strasse

Do not go into the furious
    Street alert with curious eyes;
Shield yourself from the injurious
    Glances that no men disguise.

Everything that's good befriends you,
    Till I, burning in suspense,
Watch while even laughter lends you
    Lovely arts of innocence.

Yet, in some repeated dream, I
    Know, though you seem born to bless,
You, so good, will come to be my
    Bosomful of bitterness.

Überall, wo du auch wandelst

I am helpless. You defeat me
    Everywhere and every hour;
And the more that you mistreat me
    All the more I'm in your power.

Cruelty makes me surrender.
    So, if you should tire of me,
Give me love; grow kind and tender –
    That's the way to set me free.

Es kommt zu spät, was du mir lächelst

Too late your sighs and smiles of promise,
    Your little hints of love, too late.
Emotion's dead. The pulse is quiet
    That beat at such an anxious rate.

Too late the thought of mutual passion;
    Too late the talk of being brave.
Your ardent look is no more rousing
    Than sunlight falling on a grave.

This would I know: When life is over
    Where can the tired spirit go?
Where is the fire that we extinguished?
    Where is the wind that ceased to blow?

YOLANDA AND MARIE

Diese Damen, sie verstehen

Both of them know how to honor
    Poets; they do not discuss
Art. Instead, they give me luncheon,
    Me and my great genius.

Ah! The soup was most auspicious,
    And the wine increased the mood;
The roast chicken was delicious,
    And the larded hare was good.

And the Muse? We dined upon her,
    Full to tears, and loath to part;
And I thanked them for the honor
    They had shown me and my Art.

In welche soll ich mich verlieben

Which of them shall I fall in love with?
    Both of them make my senses swirl.
The mother's still a lovely woman;
    The daughter's an enchanting girl.

In those young arms and virgin beauties
   My trembling heart is almost caught!
But thrilling too are genial glances
   That understand each casual thought.

My heart resembles our gray brother,
   Who stands, a jackass self-confessed,
Between two bundles of his fodder,
   Uncertain which may taste the best.

Die Flaschen sind leer, das Frühstück war gut

The bottles are empty, the breakfast was good,
   The ladies are gay as at night;
They pull off their corsets (I knew that they would);
   I think they are just a bit tight.

The shoulders – how white! The young breasts – how neat!
   I stand, like the dumbest of lovers.
They throw themselves down on the bed's snowy sheet,
   And, giggling, dive under the covers.

They draw the bed-curtains; I watch them prepare
   To shed the last wisp of their clothing,
And there, like the fool of the world, I stare
   At the foot of the bed, and do nothing.

Jugend, die mir täglich schwindet

Youth is leaving me; but daily
　By new courage it's replaced;
And my bold arm circles gaily
　Many a young and slender waist.

Some were shocked and others pouted;
　Some grew wroth — but none denied.
Flattery has always routed
　Lovely shame and stubborn pride.

Yet the best is gone. Too late, I'd
　Give my soul for it, in truth.
Can it be the blundering, great-eyed,
　Sweet stupidity of youth?

KATHARINE

Den Tag, den hab' ich so himmlisch verbracht

I spent the day in a heavenly way;
　Evening still found me elated.
We dined and wined; Kitty was kind;
　And love remained unsated.

The red lips warmed and pleaded and stormed;
    Hot and wild were her hands;
The brown eyes yearned, the bosom burned
    With ever-increasing demands.

She held me fast, and only at last
    I slipped the amorous tether,
In the living snare of her own bright hair
    I tied her hands together.

Du liegst mir so gern im Arme

You lie in my arms so gladly,
    The cries of the world seem far.
I am your own dear heaven,
    You are my dearest star.

Below us the foolish people
    Quibble and quarrel and fight;
They shriek and bellow and argue.
    And all of them are right.

With jingling bells on their fool's caps,
    They rise from their stupid beds;
Swinging their clubs in anger,
    They crack each other's heads.

But we, we two are lucky
That they are all so far –
You bury in its white heaven
Your head, my dearest star.

Unsre Seelen bleiben freilich

Our platonic souls are surely
In a state of rare perfection,
Firm as faith, upheld securely
By some spiritual connection.

And, though spirits slip their tether
It would not be such a bother,
For our souls have wings of ether
And they soon would find each other.

Spirits likewise are immortal,
And Eternity's untiring;
Anyone with time and patience
Can achieve the heart's desiring.

Yet our bodies are but bodies;
Arms they have which we must cherish;
Quite devoid of wings of ether,
They have mortal legs, and perish.

Think of this, and so take pity;
  Do not lift one restless feather
Till the spring, my clever Kitty,
  When we'll fly away together.

Ich liebe solche weisse Glieder

I love this white and slender body,
  These limbs that answer love's caresses,
Passionate eyes, and forehead covered
  With a wave of thick, black tresses.

You are the very one I've searched for
  In many lands, in every weather.
You are my sort; you understand me;
  As equals we can talk together.

215

In me you've found the man you care for.
And, for a while, you'll richly pay me
With kindness, kisses, and endearments –
And then, as usual, you'll betray me.

Jüngstens träumte mir: Spazieren

Once I dreamed that I went walking
Up and down the streets of Heaven,
She with me; for, lacking Kitty,
Heaven itself were Purgatory.

There I saw the chosen spirits,
The most pious and the saintly,
Those who, when they lived as mortals,
Starved the flesh to serve the spirit.

Churchmen, patriarchs, apostles,
Self-denying monks and hermits,
Hideous graybeards, youthful zealots,
And the young ones were the ugliest.

Pale, attenuated faces,
Grim ascetics, strictly tonsured,
(Various Jews were there among them)
Passed us, frowning circumspectly,

Seeing nothing, eyes averted,
Although you, my ever-lovely,
Pressed my arm and hung upon me,
Hung upon me, laughing, teasing.

One alone looked straight upon you,
And it was the only handsome
Man in the entire assembly,
And his face was wonder-working.

Lips were molded by compassion,
Eyes were carved with understanding,
As once on the Magdalene,
Now he looked, looked long upon you.

Oh! I know how well he meant it —
No one is so pure and holy —
But (I might as well admit it)
Jealous anger burned within me.

And I must confess, in Heaven
Heaven itself grew hateful to me,
Irritated — God forgive me! —
By our Saviour, Jesus Christ.

A GARLAND OF GIRLS

Gesanglos war ich und beklommen

Songless I was, immersed in mourning,
   Now song, at last, the gloom disperses;
Like tears that come with never a warning
   So, without warning, come the verses.

Once more melodic strains are starting
   To sing of great love, greater anguish,
Of hearts that have to break at parting,
   And hearts that only live to languish.

Sometimes I feel mysterious fleetings,
   And German oaks about me glimmer;
They hint of home and early meetings –
   But they are dreams, and they grow dimmer.

Sometimes it seems I hear them singing,
   Remembered German nightingales!
In jets of song the notes are springing –
   But they are dreams; the music fails.

Where are the roses, those bright vagrants,
   In German fields? They rise and haunt me
Though they are withered, ghostly fragrance.
   In dreams they bloom, in dreams they taunt me.

KITTY

Er ist so herzbeweglich

Her letter leaves me breathless.
   She says (at least she writes me)
   Her love, that so delights me,
Is timeless, speechless, deathless.

She's bored and dull and sickly
   And never will recover
   Unless..."You must come over
To England, yes – and quickly!"

Es läuft dahin die Barke

Swift as a deer, my bark
   Cuts through the waters, leaping
   Over the Thames, and sweeping
Us on to Regents' Park.

There lives my darling Kitty,
   Whose love is never shoddy;
   Who has the whitest body
In West End of the City.

219

She smiles, expecting me there,
 And fills the water-kettle,
 And wheels the tiny settle
Forward – and we have tea there!

Das Glück, das gestern mich geküsst

The joy that kissed me yesterday
 Has disappeared already;
Long years ago I found it so:
 True love is never steady.

Oft curiosity has drawn
 Some lovely ladies toward me;
But when they looked deep in my heart
 They left, and then abhorred me.

Some have grown pale before they went,
 And some with laughter cleft me;
But only Kitty really cared –
 She wept before she left me.

JENNY

Ich bin nun fünfunddreissig Jahr' alt

My years now number five-and-thirty
   And you are scarce fifteen, you sigh...
Yet, Jenny, when I look upon you,
   The old dream wakes that will not die.

In eighteen-seventeen a maiden
   Became my sweetheart, fond and true;
Strangely like yours her form and features,
   She even wore her hair like you.

That year, before I left for college,
   I said, "My own, it will not be
Long till I come back home. Be faithful!"
   "You are my world," she answered me.

Three years I toiled; three years I studied;
   And then – it was the first of May –
In Göttingen the tidings reached me:
   My love had married and gone away.

It was the first of May! With laughter
   The spring came dancing through the world.
Birds sang, and in the quickening sunshine
   Worms stretched themselves and buds uncurled.

And only I grew pale and sickly,
    Dead to all beauties and delights;
And only God knows how I suffered
    And lived throughout those wretched nights.

But still I lived. And now my health is
    Strong as an oak that seeks the sky.
Yet, Jenny, when I look upon you,
    The old dream wakes that will not die.

IN EXILE

Ich hatte einst ein schönes Vaterland

I had, long since, a lovely Fatherland.
    The oaks would gleam
And touch the skies; the violets would nod.
    It was a dream.

You'd kiss me, and in German you would say
  (Oh, joy supreme –
How sweet the sound of it!) "*Ich liebe dich*"...
  It was a dream.

BALLADS

~~~~~~~~~~~~~~~~~~~~~

TRAGEDY

1

Entflieh mit mir und sei mein Weib

"Oh, fly with me and be my love,
  Rest on my heart, and never rouse;
  And in strange lands my heart shall be
  Thy Fatherland and father's house.

"But if you stay, then I die here,
  And you shall weep and wring your hands;
  And even in your father's house
  You shall be living in strange lands."

2

Es fiel ein Reif in der Frühlingsnacht

The hoar-frost fell on a night in spring,
It fell on the young and tender blossoms.
And they have withered and perished.

A boy and a girl were once in love;
They fled from the house into the world –
They told neither father nor mother.

They wandered here and they wandered there;
They had neither luck nor a star for guide.
And they have withered and perished.

3

Auf ihrem Grab da steht eine Linde

Upon their grave a tree stands now
With winds and birds in every bough;
And in the green place under it
The miller's boy and his sweetheart sit.

The winds grow tender, soft and clinging,
And softly birds begin their singing.
The prattling sweethearts grow silent and sigh,
And fall to weeping, neither knows why.

A WOMAN

Sie hatten sich beide so herzlich lieb

They loved each other beyond belief —
She was a strumpet, he was a thief;
Whenever she thought of his tricks, thereafter
She'd throw herself on the bed with laughter.

The day was spent with a reckless zest;
All night she lay upon his breast.
So when they took him, a moment after
She watched at the window, with laughter.

He sent word, pleading, "Oh, come to me,
I need you, need you bitterly,
Yes, here and in the hereafter."
Her little head shook with laughter.

At six in the morning they swung him high;
At seven the turf on his grave was dry;
At eight the same day she quaffed her
Red wine, and sang with laughter!

THE ADJURATION

Der junge Franziskaner sitzt

The young Franciscan sits alone
Within his cloister-cell;
He reads a book of magic called
"The Mastery of Hell."

Then, as the midnight hour strikes,
He raves and calls upon
The powers of the underworld,
And cries, distraught and wan:

"For this one night, you spirits, raise
From all the hosts that died
The fairest woman – give her life,
And place her at my side."

He breathes the aweful, secret word;
And, answering his commands,
In white and drooping cerements
The perished Beauty stands.

Her face is sad. With frightened sighs
Her poor, cold breasts are stirred.
She sits beside the startled monk.
They stare – without a word.

ANNO 1829

Dass ich bequem verbluten kann

Give me a nobler, wider sphere
    Where I, at least, can bleed to death.
Oh, do not let me stifle here
    Among these hucksters. Give me breath!

They eat and drink with greedy pride,
    Dull and complacent as the mole;
Their generosity is wide —
    As wide as, say, the poor-box hole.

Cigar in mouth they stroll along;
    Their hands are fat with many a gem;
Their stomachs are both huge and strong.
    But who could ever stomach *them*!

They deal in spices, but the air
    Is filled, alas, with something else;
Their souls pollute the atmosphere,
    And foul it with their fishy smells.

If they but had some human vice,
    Some lust too terrible to see —
But not these virtues, not this nice
    Flabby and smug morality.

Ye clouds above, take me away
    To Africa or furthest North;
Even to Pomerania. Pray
    Carry me with you, bear me forth.

Take me away . . . They pass me by.
    The clouds are wise; they do not heed.
For when they see this town, they fly
    And anxiously increase their speed.

ANNO 1839

O Deutschland, meine ferne Liebe

O Germany, for which I weary,
    Thinking of you, I have to weep;
This merry France grows somehow dreary,
    These light folks put my mind to sleep.

Reason alone, dry and unfeeling,
    Is crowned in every Paris street —
O bells of home! O happy pealing!
    O faith so foolish, and so sweet!

These courtly manners! I distrust 'em!
    The mincing bow, the formal kiss!
The German peasant's rudest custom
    Means more to me than all of this.

These grinning ladies' endless clatter:
　　A mill-wheel grinding in each head!
Give me the girls, who, without chatter,
　　Smile and go quietly to bed.

Here, round and round in frantic motion,
　　All things are whirled, a headlong race.
There everything's nailed down with caution,
　　And stays in its appointed place.

Somewhere at home the muted blowing
　　Of a night-watchman's horn prevails;
There his nocturnal song is growing
　　And mingling with the nightingale's.

That was the poet's native clime, with
　　Sheltering oaks on Schilda's heath.
'Twas there I wove the happy rhyme with
　　Moonbeam-light and violet breath.

THE UNKNOWN

Meiner goldgelockten Schönen

My adored and golden-haired one,
Every day I'm sure to meet her,
When beneath the chestnut branches
In the Tuileries she wanders.

Every day she comes and walks there
With two old and awful ladies.
Are they aunts? Or are they dragons?
Or dragoons in skirts and flounces?

No one even seems to know her.
I have asked friends and relations;
But I ask in vain. I question,
While I almost die of longing.

Yes, I'm frightened by the grimness
Of her two mustached companions;
And I'm even more upset by
This, my heart's unusual beating.

I have scarcely breathed a whisper
Or a sigh whene'er I passed her;
I have never dared a burning
Glance to tell her of my longing.

But today I have discovered
What her name is. It is Laura;
Like the sweet Italian maiden
Worshiped by the famous poet.

She is Laura! I'm as great now
As was Petrarch when he chanted
And extolled his lovely lady
In those canzonets and sonnets.

She is Laura! Yes, like Petrarch,
I can hold platonic revels
With this name, and clasp its beauty –
He, himself, did nothing more.

BALLADS

〰〰〰〰〰〰〰

PSYCHE

In der Hand die kleine Lampe

With a small lamp in her fingers
    And a great glow in her breast,
Psyche creeps into the chamber
    Where the sleeper is at rest.

She grows frightened and she blushes
    As she sees his beauty bare –
While the god of love awakens,
    And his pinions beat the air.

Eighteen hundred years of penance!
    She, poor soul, still fasts with awe;
Almost dead, because she came where
    Love lay naked – and she saw!

DAME METTE
(From the Danish)

Herr Peter und Bender sassen beim Wein

As Peter and Bender sat at their wine,
    Sir Bender said brusquely, "I fear you
Are wasting your voice. Though the world rejoice,
    Dame Mette will never hear you."

Sir Peter replied, "I'll wager my horse
    Against your dogs, that I'll sing her
Into my bed." He smiled and said,
  "This very night I'll bring her."

And as the hour of midnight struck,
    Sir Peter began his singing.
His voice was good, over water and wood
    The notes went roundly ringing.

The gossiping pines were suddenly still;
    The stream, that babbler and lisper,
Grew silent soon; the inquisitive moon
    And the stars forgot to whisper.

It woke Dame Mette out of her sleep.
  "Who sings this song of wooing?"
She threw on a dress, nor stopped to guess
    What mischief might be brewing.

Over the water and through the wood
    With a purpose blind and tragic
She hurried along; Sir Peter's song
    Drew her with its dark magic.

And when she returned at early morn
    Sir Bender arose and met her.
"Where spent you this night? If I see aright
    You are wet and your clothes are wetter."

"Oh, I have been to the nixies' pool
   To hear their prophesying.
Dancing so free, they spattered me,
   And there's been no time for drying."

"The sand at the nixies' pool is fine,
   And soft is the path that's leading
From here to there; but bloody and bare
   Are your feet, and your cheeks are bleeding."

"Last night I was in the elfinwood
   To watch the fairy dances.
A thorn or two – What is it to you?
   I went and took my chances."

"The elves do dance, but only in May,
   And on a carpet of flowers,
But this is fall. The cold winds call
   And leaves come down in showers."

"I was – I was with Sir Peter last night;
   He sang, and his song was magic.
Through water and wood, careless of blood
   I went, though the end is tragic.

"His song is powerful as death;
   The notes still echo through me,
Who now must learn what makes them burn
   And why they turn to doom me."

They've hung the old church-door with black;
　　Thickly the crowds are massing;
The organ rolls, the one bell tolls;
　　Dame Mette's soul is passing.

Sir Bender weeps beside the bier;
　　His cries make a doleful jargon:
"Oh, woe betide, I've lost my bride
　　And my good hounds in the bargain."

A MEETING

Wohl unter der Linde erklingt die Musik

Under the linden the music is gay,
　　The couples are gossiping loudly;
And two are dancing whom nobody knows,
　　They carry themselves so proudly.

Now here, now there, they glide and sway
　　In wave-like measures beguiling.
They bow to each other, and as they nod,
　　She whispers, gently smiling:

"A water-pink is hanging from
　　Your cap, my fair young dancer;
It only grows in the depths of the sea –
　　You are no mortal man, sir.

"You are a merman, and to lure
  These village maids your wish is.
I knew you at once by your watery eyes
  And your teeth as sharp as the fishes'."

Now here, now there, they glide and sway
  In wave-like measures beguiling.
They bow to each other, and as they nod,
  He answers, gently smiling:

"My lovely lady, tell me why
  Your hand's so cold and shiny?
And why is the border of your gown
  So damp and draggled and briny?

"I knew you at once by your watery eyes.
  And your bow so mocking and tricksy –
You're not a daughter of earth, my dear;
  You are my cousin, the nixie."

The fiddles are silent, the dancing is done;
  They part with a ripple of laughter.
They know each other too well and will try
  To avoid such a meeting hereafter.

KING HAROLD HARFAGER

Der König Harald Harfager

The good King Harold Harfager
    Lies in the depths below;
His water-witch beside him,
    He sees time come and go.

Held in the lovely mermaid's arms
    He neither lives nor dies;
Resigned to his delicious doom,
    Two hundred years he lies.

The King's head rests in the mermaid's lap;
    His dark eyes strain above;
Yearning to meet her burning eyes,
    He cannot look enough.

His golden hair is silver-gray,
    His yellow face forlorn;
On ghostly cheeks the bones stand out,
    The skin is withered and torn.

Yet sometimes from his dream of love
    King Harold suddenly wakes;
He hears the billows roaring above
    While his crystal palace shakes.

Sometimes it seems to him the wind
   Throbs with the Norsemen's call;
Swiftly he lifts his battle arm,
   Then sadly lets it fall.

Sometimes he thinks he hears the chant
   Of sailors crude and strong,
Praising King Harold Harfager
   In some heroic song.

Then groans the King, and wails and weeps,
   His bosom pierced with pain...
The water-witch leans over his mouth
   And kisses him quiet again.

DOCTRINE

Schlage die Trommel und fürchte dich nicht

Beat on the drum and blow the fife
And kiss the *vivandière*, my boy.
Fear nothing – that's the whole of life,
Its deepest truth, its soundest joy.

240

Beat reveillè, and with a blast
    Arouse all men to valiant strife.
Waken the world; and then, at last,
    March on ... That is the whole of life.

This is philosophy; this is truth;
    This is the burning source of joy!
I've borne this wisdom from my youth,
    For I, too, was a drummer-boy.

A WARNING

Solche Bücher lässt du drucken!

You will print such books as these?
    Then you're lost, my friend, that's certain.
    If you wish for gold and honor,
Write more humbly; bend your knees.

Yes, you must have lost your senses,
    Thus to speak before the people,
    Thus to dare to talk of preachers
And of potentates and princes.

Friend, you're doomed, so it appears;
    For the princes have long arms,
    And the preachers have long tongues,
And the masses have long ears!

ADAM THE FIRST

Du schicktest mit dem Flammenschwert

With flaming swords You sent police
    Down from The Heavenly City,
And drove me out of Eden's walls
    With neither right nor pity.

Now with my wife I journey forth,
    Through further country ranging;
Yet I have eaten wisdom's fruit —
    A fact beyond Your changing.

You cannot change my mind that knows
    How small You are. I wonder
Whether You hope to make yourself
    Great with mere death and thunder.

I will not miss Your Paradise
    Miraculously hidden;
Eden is scarcely worth the name
    Where some things are forbidden.

I ask for freedom's fullest rights
    Now freedom's star has risen;
Otherwise Heaven becomes a hell,
    And Paradise a prison.

THE TENDENCY

Deutscher Sänger! Sing und preise

German singers! sing and praise
　　German freedom, till your song
　　　　Makes the heart leap up to hear it,
　　　　And the deed supports the spirit,
Like the stirring Marseillaise.

Turn from Werther and his wooing –
　　For his Lotte let him long!
　　　　Peal the bell and strike the hour.
　　　　Now the people come to power,
Sword in hand, aroused and doing.

Do not sigh, "What does it matter?"
　　Like a love-sick flute. Be strong.
　　　　Be a trumpet! Be the thunder!
　　　　Be the charge that tears asunder!
Crash and conquer, blow and shatter!

A PROMISE

Nicht mehr barfuss sollst du traben

Freedom, stumbling through the stews,
 Barefoot, spat upon, and shocking,
Cheer up! Some day you'll have shoes,
 And perhaps (who knows?) a stocking.

Freedom, some day you will wear
 A warm cap with ear-laps showing;
Then you will not have to care
 In the path of all winds blowing.

Men will nod to you, no less;
 They may even house and feed you;
They may love you to excess,
 But, of course, they will not heed you.

You, however, must, you see,
 Listen to your lords *and* heed 'em.
Hold your tongue and bend your knee,
 And you'll have a future, Freedom.

NIGHT THOUGHTS

Denk ich an Deutschland in der Nacht

Nights when I think of Germany
Sleep is impossible for me;
Tear upon tear so hotly flows
My burning eyes refuse to close.

The years have come, the years have gone;
Twelve years now since an ailing son
Has seen his mother. At the thought
My heart sinks and my nerves grow taut.

My longing mounts to fever-pitch.
That woman – can she be a witch?
As I grow older, love grows deeper
For that old lady, may God keep her.

That frail old lady loves me so
It troubles me. Her letters show
How pitifully the poor hand trembles
And how the mother-heart dissembles.

Germany's an immortal land;
Sound to the core, it's sure to stand.
Its oaks and lindens will survive
And keep the homeward heart alive.

But I could wait; I would not wear
My heart away were she not there.
The Fatherland is deathless, aye;
But that poor soul is bound to die.

Since I forsook the German sun
So many friends are dead and gone;
If I should stop to count the roll
I would be sickened to the soul.

Yet count I must, although the count
Reaches a shuddering amount.
The dead press on me, even here,
Until (thank God!) they disappear.

Thank God! Upon my windows dance
Dawn and the happy light of France.
My wife comes in with morning gladness,
And smiles away my German sadness.

THE WEAVERS

Im düstern Auge keine Träne

From darkened eyes no tears are falling;
With gritted teeth we sit here calling:
"Germany, listen, ere we disperse,
We weave your shroud with a triple curse –
We weave! We are weaving!

"A curse to the false god that we prayed to,
And worshipped in spite of all, and obeyed, too.
We waited, and hoped, and suffered in vain;
He laughed at us, sneering, for all of our pain –
We weave! We are weaving!

"A curse to the king, and a curse to his coffin,
The rich man's king whom our plight could not soften;
Who took our last penny by taxes and cheats,
And let us be shot like dogs in the streets –
We weave! We are weaving!

"A curse to the Fatherland, whose face is
Covered with lies and foul disgraces;
Where the bud is crushed before it can seed,
And the worm grows fat on corruption and greed –
We weave! We are weaving!

"The shuttle flies in the creaking loom;
And night and day we weave your doom.
Old Germany, listen, ere we disperse,
We weave your shroud with a triple curse.
We weave! We are weaving!"

TWO SONGS

Wir müssen zugleich uns betrüben

We laugh and we are troubled
   Whene'er our fingers touch,
That hearts can love so greatly
   And minds can doubt so much.

Do you not feel, my darling,
   My heart beat through the gloom?
She nods her head, and murmurs,
   "It beats – God knows for whom!"

Das macht den Menschen glücklich

It makes a man feel happy,
   It drains him to the dregs,
When he has three fair sweethearts
   And just one pair of legs.

I visit the first in the morning;
   I seek the second at night;
The third does not wait, but comes to me
   At noon in a blaze of light.

Farewell, my three fair sweethearts,
   Two legs are all I've got;
I'll go and make love to Nature
   In some more quiet spot.

vvvvvvvvvvvvvvvvvvvv

CHARLES I

Im Wald, in der Köhlerhütte sitzt

In a wood, in a charcoal-burner's hut,
    Far from his lordly city,
A poor king rocks a poor man's child,
    Singing a nursery ditty:

Eya-popeya, what stirs in the straw?
    The sheep in their stalls are bleating –
O child, your face, the look on your brow,
    Is a thing that my dreams keep repeating.

Eya-popeya, the kitten is dead –
    It's a look that needs no dissembling.
You'll soon be a man, and you'll swing an ax.
    Already the oaks are trembling.

The charcoal-burner's faith is dead;
The children no longer are loyal –
Eya-popeya – to God or to king,
Despising the old blood-royal.

The kitten is dead; the mice can play –
We are doomed in lowland and highland –
Eya-popeya – in Heaven the Lord,
And I, the King, on his island.

My courage is gone; my heart is sick;
No single hope besteads me –
Eya-popeya – an arm like yours
Will swing the ax that beheads me.

My death-song is your cradle-song . . .
I feel the short hair bristling –
Eya-popeya – I hear the blade
Swiftly and horribly whistling.

Eya-popeya, what stirs in the straw?
The ax falls – dead is the kitten –
My head leaps from the startled trunk.
'Tis you who will rule in Britain.

Eya-popeya, what stirs in the straw?
The sheep in their stalls huddle neatly.
The kitten is dead; the mice can play.
Sleep, little headsman, sleep sweetly.

THE ASRA

Täglich ging die wunderschöne

Daily came the lone and lovely
Sultan's daughter, slowly wandering
In the evening to the fountain
Where the plashing waters whitened.

Daily stood the youthful captive
In the evening by the fountain
Where the plashing waters whitened –
Daily growing pale and paler.

Till one dusk the strolling Princess
Stopped, and suddenly addressed him:
"Tell me now thy name, and tell me
Of thy country and thy kindred."

And the slave replied, "My name is
Mòhamet; I come from Yemen.
And my people are the Asra,
Who, whene'er they love, must perish."

AMERICA
(From "Vitzliputzli")

Dieses ist Amerika!

This is America!
This is the new world!
Not the present European
Wasted and withering sphere.

This is the new world,
As it was when Columbus
Drew it first from the ocean.
Radiant with its freshening bath;

Still dripping its watery pearls,
In showers and spurts of color
As the light of the sun kisses them.
How strong and healthy is this world!

This is no graveyard of romance;
This is no pile of ruins,
Of fossilized wigs and symbols
Or stale and musty tradition!

Out of healthy ground there blossom
Healthy flowers – not a creature
In that land's blasé, or suffers
Rotting of the spinal marrow...

A new country! New the fervor,
New the flowers, new the fragrance!
Here the very air is heady
With invigorating perfumes!

A VISIT HOME

(From "Germany: A Winter Fairy-Tale")

Von Harburg fuhr ich in einer Stund'

I drove from Harburg – an easy hour –
    As evening came to calm me,
Welcomed by each familiar star;
    The air was kind and balmy.

And when my mother saw me, she
    Clung to me with excitement;
She cried, clasped hands, and stared at me,
    Not sure just what the flight meant.

254

"My poor child! For these thirteen years
 In France you've had to live; you
Need a good meal, you must be starved.
 Sit down. What can I give you?

"There's fish at home, and there is goose,
 And oranges sweet as honey."
"Good. I'll have fish, and I'll have goose,
 And oranges warm and sunny."

And as I ate, my mother glowed;
 She crowed at my good digestion.
And then, alas, she embarrassed me
 With question after question.

"Do you live well in your home abroad?
 Are all your troubles ended?
Does your wife know how to run the house?
 Are your shirts and socks well mended?"

"The fish is excellent, mother, my own,
 But the bones are a terrible bother;
I'd hate to have one lodge in my throat,
 So let me alone, dear mother."

As soon as I had disposed of the fish,
 The goose was brought to the table.
She asked about that, and she asked about this,
 As soon as she was able.

"Dear child, do you prefer the French
  Or Germans? Or do you waver?
Is France a pleasanter place than this?
  And which is the land you favor?"

"This German goose is wonderful;
  But, mother, the French have powers
Uncanny, it seems, when it comes to a sauce,
  And their stuffing is better than ours."

After the goose was wholly consumed
  The oranges weren't neglected;
I found them ripe and juicy and sweet,
  Far sweeter than I expected.

And then my mother began again
  With many a curious glance; her
Questions came tumbling; and all in vain
  I sought for the ready-made answer.

"My child, I'm anxious to hear you name
  Your political predilections.
What is your party? What is its aim?
  And what are your own convictions?"

"It was most delicious, mother, my own;
  The oranges really were fine, dear.
I enjoyed the juice to the last sweet drop,
  But I'll leave the bitter rind here."

256

GOOD-FORTUNE AND BAD-LUCK

Das Glück ist eine leichte Dirne

Good-Fortune is a giddy maid,
  Fickle and restless as a fawn;
She smooths your hair; and then the jade
  Kisses you quickly, and is gone.

But Madam Bad-Luck scorns all this,
  She shows no eagerness for flitting;
But with a long and fervent kiss
  Sits by your bed – and brings her knitting.

TAKE UP THE LYRE

Wenn man an dir Verrat geübt

When a false world betrays your trust
  And stamps upon your fire,
When what seemed blood is only rust,
  Take up the lyre.

How quickly the heroic mood
  Responds to its own ringing;
The scornful heart, the angry blood,
  Leap upward, singing!

257

THE MORNING AFTER

Diese graue Wolkenschar

These gray clouds, so thickly strewn,
  Rose from golden skies and gay;
Yesterday I called the tune,
  And today I have to pay.

Ah, the nectar of last night
  Turns to wormwood. Such is fate!
And the head that was so light
  Cannot even hold its weight.

RETROSPECT

Ich habe gerochen alle Gerüche

I have smelled every one of the thousand smells
In earth's warm kitchens, have drunk from the wells
Of a thousand pleasures; the great and small
Delights of the world, I have tasted them all.
I've drunk good coffee, have eaten buns;
Have fondled dolls – and the loveliest ones;
Have worn silk vests and the finest hose;
I've even had money in my clothes.
I've ridden a high horse with silver tassels;
I've had fine houses, have lived in castles;

I've thought of myself as a favorite one
Caressed by the golden kiss of the sun;
My brow was crowned with a wreath of laurel,
And I dreamed sweet dreams with never a moral,
Dreams of a soft and endless May,
Where the spirit was free and life's purpose was play,
Never a darkness, disease, nor drouth –
Roast pigeons flew in my open mouth;
Angels distributed golden ducats
And champagne flasks from their inside pockets.
Ah, these were visions, bright soap-bubbles.
They burst . . . And, now, beset with troubles,
I lie in a damp and draughty attic;
My head is heavy, my limbs rheumatic;
All of me withered, crippled, and lame,
The once-proud spirit broken with shame.
For each quick pleasure, each joyful vice
I've paid full measure – and often twice.
I've drowned in bitterness, burned in ice,
Been bled by friends and bitten by lice;
I've been attended by blackest sorrow;
I've had to lie, I've had to borrow
From rich young fools and be beholden,
Like a common beggar, to a crusty old 'un.
But now I am tired; I long to sleep
In a new-made bed that's dark and deep.
Farewell. I know, my Christian brother,
In Heaven (alas) we will see each other.

SOLOMON

Verstummt sind Pauken, Posaunen und Zinken

The trumpets and drums no longer are sounded,
  Hushed is the dulcimer and flute.
  King Solomon sleeps, and the night is mute.
He sleeps, by twelve thousand angels surrounded.

They guard his dreams from clamor and cumber.
  And should he even knit his brow
  Twelve thousand arms would be lifted now,
Twelve thousand swords would flash through his slumber.

Yet gently now the swords are lying
  Within each scabbard. The night-winds soothe
  The dreamer's dreams and his brow is smooth;
Only his lips are restless, sighing:

"O Shulamite! all people cherish
  My favor, and bring me tributes, and sing;
  I am both Judah's and Israel's king.
But, lacking your love, I wither and perish."

ENFANT PERDU

Verlor'ner Posten in dem Freiheitskriege

For more than thirty years I've been defending,
  In freedom's struggle, many a desperate post.
I knew the fight was hopeless, never-ending;
  But still I fought, wounded and battle-tossed.

Waking through nights and days, no peaceful slumbers
  Were mine while all the others slept their fill.
(The mighty snoring of these valiant numbers
  Kept me awake when I was tired or ill.)

In those long nights I have been often frightened,
  For only fools are not afraid of fear,
But I would whistle till the terror lightened,
  And sing my mocking rhymes to give me cheer.

Yes, I have stood, my musket primed and ready,
  On guard; and when some rascal raised his head
I took good aim, my arm was always steady,
  And let him have a bellyfull of lead.

And yet those knaves – I may as well admit it –
  Could shoot quite well; the rascals often chose
A splendid mark, and, what is more, they hit it.
  My wounds are gaping, and the blood still flows.

One post is vacant! As a bloody token
I wear my wounds. Another takes my part.
But, though I fall, my sword is still unbroken;
The only thing that's broken is my heart.

THIS VALE OF TEARS

Der Nachtwind durch die Luken pfeift

The windows shake, the whistling gale
Tries panes loose and unleaded;
And in the attic, poor and pale,
Two freezing souls are bedded.

One speaks: "These are but vain alarms.
What though the world is stormy,
Your mouth on mine is sweet, your arms
Are all I need to warm me."

The other, whispering, replies:
"Such moments make us stronger;
For when I look into your eyes
There is no cold nor hunger."

They laugh and hold each other fast,
Their kisses have no number;
They weep and sing, and then at last
Fall into wordless slumber.

Next day there came the coroner
  And, doctor, widely cherished;
And both of them agreed 'twas clear
  That the poor souls had perished.

"An empty stomach," they averred,
  "Combined with bitter weather
Hastened the death which here occurred,
  Or caused it altogether.

"When cold sets in one must withstand
  The weather; we've discovered
It's best to be well-nourished and
  To lie in bed well-covered."

THE SONG OF SONGS

Des Weibes Leib ist ein Gedicht

Woman's white body is a song,
  And God Himself's the author;
In the eternal book of life
  He put the lines together.

It was a thrilling hour; the Lord
  Felt suddenly inspired;
Within his brain the stubborn stuff
  Was mastered, fused, and fired.

Truly, the Song of Songs is this,
  The greatest of his trophies:
This living poem where white limbs
  Are a rare pair of strophes.

Oh, what a heavenly masterpiece
  That neck and its relation
To the fair head, like an idea
  Crowned with imagination.

In pointed epigrams, the breasts
  Rise under teasing rallies;
And a caesura lies between,
  The loveliest of valleys.

He published the sweet parallel
  Of thighs – what joy to be there!
The fig-leaf grotto joining them
  Is not a bad place either.

It is no cold, conceptual verse,
  No patterned abstract study.
This poem sings with rhyming lips,
  With sweet bones and warm body.

Here breathes the deepest poetry!
  Beauty in every motion,
Upon its brow it bears the stamp
  Of His complete devotion.

Here in the dust, I praise Thee, Lord.
We are – and well I know it –
Rank amateurs, compared to Thee:
Heaven's first major poet!

I'll dedicate myself to learn
This song, the lyric body;
With ardor and with energy
All day – and night – I'll study.

Yes, day and night, I'll never lack
For constant application;
And though the task may break my back
I'll ask for no vacation!

SONG OF THE VIVANDIÈRE

Und die Husaren lieb' ich sehr

The gay hussars – I love them all –
They are such splendid fellows;
The thin and small, the large and tall,
The blue ones and the yellows.

And then I love the musketeers –
I love them without penance;
The shy recruits, the grizzled boots,
The privates and lieutenants.

The cavalry and the infantry
  Have furnished many a lover,
And often the old artillery
  Has kept me under cover.

I love the Welsh, I love the Dutch,
  The Swedes, the French, the Germans;
I serve them all whate'er befall
  Th'upstanding and infirm 'uns.

I do not care what flag they bear;
  Whether they're poor or wealthy;
I do not care what faith they swear,
  As long as they are healthy.

Faith and the Fatherland! These are
  The shreds of outworn clothing!
Without his clothes a woman knows
  If man's a man – or nothing.

Woman and man are greater than
  Religion and its raiment!
So strip and be at one with me –
  Forget about the payment.

Laughter and youth surround my booth;
  Heaven declares good weather;
The *Malvoisie* today is free.
  Come, let's be drunk together!

TO MY RELATIONS

Sie küssten mich mit ihren falschen Lippen

They kissed me with false lips; they pledged potations
  With the sweet, sparkling juices of the vine,
  And then they poured black poison in the wine –
For this I am obliged to my relations.

They robbed me of my youth; with defamations
  They stripped my flesh from me. Now I repine,
  A pack of meager bones and weakened spine –
For this I am obliged to my relations.

The records show I am a Christian, and
   Therefore I must forgive them all, and pray
   Devoutly for their souls and wish them well,
But there are times I wish I could command
   A hearty curse. Oh, how I long to say,
   "God damn your souls, and may you rot in hell."

DYING POET

Wie langsam kriechet sie dahin

How slowly Time, the frightful snail,
   Crawls to the corner that I lie in;
While I, who cannot move at all,
   Watch from the place that I must die in.

Here in my darkened cell no hope
   Enters and breaks the gloom asunder;
I know I shall not leave this room
   Except for one that's six feet under.

Perhaps I have been dead some time;
   Perhaps my bright and whirling fancies
Are only ghosts that, in my head,
   Keep up their wild, nocturnal dances.

They well might be a pack of ghosts,
  Some sort of pagan gods or devils;
And a dead poet's skull is just
  The place they'd choose to have their revels.

Those orgies, furious and sweet,
  Come suddenly, without a warning . . .
And then the poet's cold, dead hand
  Attempts to write them down next morning.

EPILOG

Unser Grab erwärmt der Ruhm

"Glory warms us in the grave."
Nonsense. That's a silly stave.
There's a better warmth than this
Found in any cow-girl's kiss,
Though she be a thick-lipped flirt,
Though she reek of dung and dirt.
And a better warmth, I'm thinking,
Every man has found in drinking;
Lapping wine, the lucky dog,
Punch or even common grog;
Sprawling over filthy benches
With the vilest thieves and wenches
That have yet deserved a hanging;

Yes, but – living and haranguing –
Worth more envy, every one,
Than fair Thetis' noble son.

Old Pelides spoke the truth:
Richer is the poorest youth
Who's alive, than lords and ladies
And the greatest kings in Hades,
Praised in many a classic tome, or
All the heroes sung by Homer!

THESE LITTLE SONGS

Ich mache die kleinen Lieder

I make these songs that, singing
　　With all a lover's art,
Fly straight to reach you, winging
　　Themselves into your heart.

Your husband's children rally
　　(No shadows, it is true)
From meadow, wood, and valley;
　　They also run to you.

The world rewards its songsters
With smiles and sighs and tears;
But when they hear your youngsters,
People must hold their ears.

And yet – though maybe wrong stirs
This body that burns and longs –
I'd rather have made your youngsters
Than any and all of my songs.

DOMESTIC END

Es geht zu End', es ist kein Zweifel

This is the end – and just as well –
Passion has swept itself to hell.
Free of love's turmoil, pain, and din,
At last the better days begin
As domesticity comes in.
At last one can enjoy one's self
With just the proper touch of pelf;
Pamper the stomach with delight;
No longer turn and toss at night
With feverish love, but slumber warm
On a consoling wifely arm.

POTATIONS

Geleert hab' ich nach Herzenswunsch

Though it was often wild and risky,
    I gratified my heart's desire –
    A drink as full of heady fire
As a hot punch of burning whisky.

But older now, I bend the knee
    To friendship that no passion fouls,
    Friendship that warms the heart and bowels,
Like a domestic cup of tea.

FINIS

Es kommt der Tod; jetzt will ich sagen

Death brings the end; and, though I dread it,
    My tight-lipped pride is ended, too,
    And I can say: "For you, for you,
My heart has beat." There – I have said it.

The grave is dug; prepared the coffin;
    And I will slumber without rue,
    But you will weep; yes, even you
Will dream of me, remembering often.

Comfort yourself. No use pretending
  This doesn't happen everywhere.
Whatever's good, and great, and fair,
  Always will have a shabby ending.

IN THE CATHEDRAL

Des Oberkirchners Töchterlein

The sexton's daughter showed me all
  Of which the church was proud.
Around her neck she wore a shawl
  As closely as a shroud.

For a few coins I saw the cross,
  Candles, and burying-place,
Softened with age, fingered by moss –
  Then I saw Elspeth's face.

The pictures glowed with more than paint;
  The incense was enhanced;
The monstrance burned, and every saint
  In every window danced.

The sexton's daughter guided me
  Wherever I cared to go;
And in her clear eyes I could see
  More than the church could show.

Pure eyes they were, without a fleck;
But I was not misled.
The shawl had fallen from her neck
And, oh, her mouth was red!

FOR "LA MOUCHE"

Es träumte mir von einer Sommernacht

I dreamed a dream: It was a summer night.
    Pale and uncertain in a vague moon's glances,
Structures arose of Renaissance delight,
    Frail, legendary ruins of romances.

And here and there, as though with fixed intent,
    A stern and solitary Doric column
Seemed challenging the lowered firmament,
    Defying thunder, delicate but solemn.

Everywhere broken sculpture lay about:
    Doors, portals, roofs, and many a shattered gable,
Centaur and sphinx, chimeras, and a rout
    Of beasts and satyrs from the Age of Fable.

There, in an open, carved sarcophagus,
    Preserved among the parts of scattered creatures,
Intact, where everything was ruinous,
    A dead man lay with mild and suffering features.

Strong caryatides with stress and strain
    Upheld the tomb, their stony necks uprearing;
Carven upon the sides one saw a train
    Of curious figures curiously appearing.

Here the lewd pagan gods all seemed to leave
    Olympus gladly as they hotly hastened;
And here was Adam standing with his Eve,
    In fig-leaf aprons, obviously chastened.

Troy flamed again and fell in ashes. Here
    Were Helen and young Paris who possessed her.
Moses and Aaron, too, were strangely near
    With Judith, Holofernes, Haman, Esther.

Phoebus Apollo rose, and one could see
    Vulcan, and Cupid with his mother, Venus,
Pluto, and Proserpine, and Mercury,
    God Bacchus, and Priapus, and Silenus.

Besides them stood poor Balaam and his ass,
    About to speak. There, direst of all slaughters,
Abraham held young Isaac, and, alas,
    Lot came carousing with his drunken daughters.

Here you saw Salomé, who danced so well,
    Bearing the Baptist's head so lewdly given;
Here was King Satan with the hosts of Hell,
    And here was Peter with the keys of Heaven.

Then, with a change of scene, you looked upon
  Jove's lustihood and his lascivious power,
Seducing Leda as a regal swan,
  And wooing Danae with a golden shower.

Wildly Diana and her hunt went by.
  Heroic Hercules, discarding his staff,
Dressed like a woman, made the spindle fly,
  The while his brawny muscles held the distaff.

Here Sinai raised its summit, and here smiled
  Israel with his oxen, sleek and ample.
And here you saw God as a little child
  Disputing with the scholars in the Temple.

The contrast deepened, grew ironical
  With Greek light-heartedness and the God-yearning
Judaic spirit – and about them all
  The ivy tendrils' arabesques were turning.

Then as the whirling pictures filled my head,
  And the whole dream grew rich and riotous,
Then, suddenly, I knew that I was dead,
  I was the man in the sarcophagus.

Guarding my final resting-place there grew
  A tall strange flower, a flower without its fellow,
Modest, and yet its power was amorous, too;
  Its fleshy petals blue and sulphur-yellow.

276

The passion-flower they call it, and they say
  When Christ was crucified, from his fair bosom
The precious drops of martyrdom that lay
  Upon the earth became this mystic blossom.

Blood-witness, so they claim; for here one sees
  The marks when, driven out of Pilate's palace,
The torturers increased His agonies –
  All, all are in the flower's perfumed chalice.

Yes, all the Passion's properties adorn
  This bloom so innocent of pain and clamor:
The scourge, the binding rope, the crown of thorn,
  The cross, the cup, the nails, the very hammer.

Such was the flower that grew upon my grave
  And bent above my body in its coffer,
And kissed my brow and eyes, and, somehow, gave
  The healing grief that mourning women offer.

Then, like a magic vision, all things grew
  Clear and the yellow flower itself grew clearest;
For now I saw, at last, that it was you –
  You were the passion-flower, you, my dearest.

You were the flower, you, belovèd child;
  That kiss was all I needed to inform me.
No flower-lips could ever be so mild,
  No flower-tears so passionate and stormy.

My eyes were closed, but still I saw your face.
  The moon was baffling; but my spirit captured
The very gestures of your ghostly grace
  As you bent over me, intense, enraptured.

We did not speak, yet I felt every thought
  Your chaste and silent tenderness could fashion –
The spoken word is shameless, good-for-naught,
  But silence is the very flower of passion.

Soundless communion! Ecstasy supreme!
  Never was there a swifter hour, a rarer
Intimate conversation in a dream
  As in that night, woven of joy and terror.

And what we spoke of? Never ask the theme.
  What do the glow-worms glimmer to the grasses?
What are the small waves lisping to the stream?
  What does the west-wind whisper as it passes?

What makes the carbuncle and ruby burn?
  What is the reason for the scents that hover
Over the roses? What's the strange concern
  The passion-flower has for the dead lover?

I do not know how long my soul enjoyed
  That marble chest, that slumber-cooled security;
I only know that something dark destroyed
  The dream that was all peacefulness and purity.

Death, with your silent grave, you give the best
    Of endless pleasure, lavish in your giving;
Life only offers yearning without rest,
    Raw passion and the silly lust for living.

But woe is me! My peace was put to rout,
    As from without there came an overpowering
Clamor and stamping, strident shout on shout;
    I saw my timid blossom bent and cowering.

Yes, from without I heard the hateful brawl
    Of voices scolding, arguing, and jangling;
And suddenly I recognized them all –
    The figures on my marble tomb were wrangling!

Must superstitions haunt me even here?
    Must marble argue among phantom roses?
Does pagan Pan utter his shriek of fear,
    Wild with the harsh anathemas of Moses?

Oh, the same fight will rage forevermore;
    The Beautiful and Good will be at variance.
Mankind will split itself, as heretofore,
    Into two parties: Hellenes and Barbarians.

Endless their oaths and shouts – a pretty pass –
    The wind of argument made heavy weather;
The controversy grew, as Balaam's ass
    Triumphed and brayed down gods and saints together.

And while the vile hee-hawing still increased,
  All hope of peace or further sleep denying,
In sheer despair against the stupid beast,
  I, too, cried out – and woke myself with crying.

LOTUS-FLOWER

(For "La Mouche")

Wahrhaftig wir beide bilden

Truly, the two of us offer
  A pretty picture to frame.
The one has lumbago to suffer,
  The other is chronically lame.

She is an ailing kitten,
  He is as sick as a dog;
Their brains have become somewhat addled,
  And both of them live in a fog.

She thinks she's a lotus-blossom
  Whose cup will be opened soon;
And he, because of his pallor,
  Fancies that he is the moon.

The lotus-blossom uncovers
  Her being the whole night long;
But all she conceives for her trouble
  Is a metaphor and a song.

IN THE MORNING

Meine gute, liebe Frau

My beloved and loving wife,
My most kind and liberal lady,
Has prepared the early breakfast:
Rich, brown coffee; cream like satin.

And, behold the way she serves it,
Smiling, teasing, singing, tempting.
In the whole of Christendom
Never a mouth can smile so sweetly.

And her flute-like voice is heard
Only now and then from angels
Or, at all events, among the
Very choicest nightingales.

Lilies are her hands; her hair
Is a cloud of curls that frames
Her entrancing countenance,
Rosy, radiant, and flawless.

She is perfect ... Yet this morning
My own darling seems to be
Growing – or am I mistaken? –
Just a wee bit corpulent.

FOR MATHILDE

Ich war, o Lamm, als Hirt bestellt

O little lamb, take comfort; see,
I am the shepherd meant for thee.
My bread was shared with thee; I'd bring
Sweet water from the clearest spring.

When the fierce winter-storms alarmed,
Here in my bosom thou wert warmed,
Sheltered against each dread occurrence.
And when the rain beat down in torrents,
And wolf and stream and evil weather
Howled in the rocky gorge together,
Thou didst not tremble, nothing mattered.
Even when sudden lightning shattered
The tallest pine, thou still wouldst rest
Sleeping securely on my breast.

My arm grows weak, my anxious soul
Feels the approach of death. My role
As pastoral-guardian, shepherd-lover
Is done, alas. The play is over.
O God, I put back in Thy hands
The shepherd's crook, with no demands
But this: When I am laid away
Watch o'er my lamb lest she should stray
In briars and her fleece be torn.

Protect her, Lord, from every thorn
And every bog with treacherous mire.
Beneath those feet before they tire
Let the new green be quickly spread
With a blue heaven overhead.
And let her sleep, when she is fed,
Serene as when she took her rest
Sleeping securely on my breast.

ANNUAL MOURNING

Keine Messe wird man singen

There will be no whispered masses,
    There will be no songs nor crying,
None will rise to say a *Kaddish*
    On the day that I lie dying.

But the day may be a fair one.
    Then (the thought is most consoling)
With Pauline upon Montmartre
    My Mathilde will go strolling.

And perhaps she'll carry flowers,
    Immortelles, dead-white and yellow;
And her pretty eyes will moisten,
    And she'll say (in French), "Poor fellow."

I'll be living far too high
   Up in Heaven (how it rankles!)
To invite her to sit down
   And relieve her tired ankles.

Oh, my plump and breathless pigeon,
   Walking's quite unnecessary.
See – the carriages are standing
   Just outside the cemetery.

WHERE?

Wo wird einst des Wandermüden

Where will I, the wander-wearied,
   Find a haven and a shrine?
Under palms will I be buried?
   Under lindens on the Rhine?

Will I lie in desert reaches,
   Buried by a stranger's hand?
Or upon the well-loved beaches,
   Covered by the friendly sand?

284

Well, what matter! God has given
Wider spaces there than here.
And the stars that swing in Heaven
Will be lamps above my bier.

IT GOES OUT

Der Vorhang fällt, das Stück ist aus

The curtain falls; the play is done;
Ladies and gentlemen, one by one,
Go home at last. How was the play?
I heard applause as I came away.
A much-respected audience
Praised the author beyond a doubt;
But now that they have all gone hence
The house is silent, the lights are out.

But wait! A sound is heard within,
Feeble but fairly near the stage;
Perhaps the string of a violin
Has suddenly broken down with age.
Peevishly in the dark parterre
The restless rats run here and there,
And the place reeks of rancid oil.

All things grow musty; all things spoil.
The last lamp tries to stem the rout;
Then, with a sputter and sigh of doubt,
The light (that was my soul) goes out.

INDEX

OF FIRST LINES

〜〜〜〜〜〜〜〜〜〜〜

INDEX OF FIRST LINES

vvvvvvvvvvvvvvvvvvvvvvvvv

Ach, die Augen sind es wieder   PAGE *144*
Ach, ich sehne mich nach Tränen   *188*
Ach, wenn ich nur der Schemel wär'   *59*
Ach, wie schön bist du, wenn traulich   *201*
Allnächtlich im Traume seh' ich dich   *75*
Als ich auf der Reise zufällig   *89*
Als meine Grossmutter die Liese behext   *24*
Als sie mich umschlang mit zärtlichem Pressen   *140*
Am blassen Meeresstrande   *178*
Am Fenster stand die Mutter   *158*
Am fernen Horizonte   *101*
Am Kreuzweg wird begraben   *79*
Am leuchtenden Sommermorgen   *68*
An deine schneeweisse Schulter   *141*
An dem stillen Meeresstrande   *196*
Andre beten zur Madonna   *125*
Anfangs wollt' ich fast verzagen   *15*
Auf dem Berge steht die Hütte   *163*
Auf den Wällen Salamancas   *147*
Auf den Wolken ruht der Mond   *93*
Auf Flügeln des Gesanges   *43*
Auf ihrem Grab da steht eine Linde   *225*
Auf meiner Herzliebsten Äugelein   *46*

Aus alten Märchen winkt es   66
Aus meinen grossen Schmerzen   60
Aus meinen Tränen spriessen   40

Berg' und Burgen schaun herunter   14
Bist du wirklich mir so feindlich   143
Blamier mich nicht, mein schönes Kind   145

Da droben auf jenem Berge   99
Dämmernd liegt der Sommerabend   151
Das Fräulein stand am Meere   198
Das Glück, das gestern mich geküsst   220
Das Glück ist eine leichte Dirne   257
Das Herz ist mir bedrückt, und sehnlich   117
Das ist der alte Märchenwald   3
Das ist ein Brausen und Heulen   75
Das ist ein Flöten und Geigen   50
Das ist ein schlechtes Wetter   110
Das macht den Menschen glücklich   248
Das Meer erglänzte weit hinaus   99
Das Meer hat seine Perlen   182
Dass ich bequem verbluten kann   228
Dass ich dich liebe, o Möpschen   19
Das weiss Gott, wo sich die tolle   139
Dein Angesicht, so lieb und schön   41
Deine weissen Lilienfinger   111
Denk ich an Deutschland in der Nacht   245
Den König Wiswamitra   121
Den Tag, den hab' ich so himmlisch verbracht   212
Der Abend kommt gezogen   96
Der arme Peter wankt vorbei   23
Der bleiche, herbstliche Halbmond   108
Der Brief, den du geschrieben   193
Der Hans und die Grete tanzen herum   22
Der Herbstwind rüttelt die Bäume   76
Der junge Franziskaner sitzt   227
Der König Harald Harfager   238
Der kranke Sohn und die Mutter   161
Der Mond ist aufgegangen   93
Der Nachtwind durch die Luken pfeift   262

Der Schmetterling ist in die Rose verliebt 185
Der Sturm spielt auf zum Tanze 96
Der Tod, das ist die kühle Nacht 150
Der Traumgott bracht' mich in ein Riesenschloss 77
Der Vorhang fällt, das Stück ist aus 285
Der Wind zieht seine Hosen an 95
Des Oberkirchners Töchterlein 273
Des Weibes Leib ist ein Gedicht 263
Deutscher Sänger! Sing und preise 243
Die alten bösen Lieder 82
Die blauen Veilchen der Äugelein 56
Die Erde war so lange geizig 55
Die Flaschen sind leer, das Frühstück war gut 211
Die heil'gen drei Könige aus Morgenland 115
Die holden Wünsche blühen 194
Die Jahre kommen und gehen 106
Die Jungfrau schläft in der Kammer 104
Die Lilie meiner Liebe 100
Die Linde blühte, die Nachtigall sang 53
Die Lotosblume ängstigt 44
Die Mitternacht war kalt und stumm 78
Die Mitternacht zog näher schon 28
Die Mutter Gottes zu Kevlaar 159
Die Nacht ist feucht und stürmisch 88
Die Rose, die Lilie, die Taube, die Sonne 40
Die schlanke Wasserlilie 188
Diese Damen, sie verstehen 210
Diese graue Wolkenschar 258
Diesen liebenswürd'gen Jüngling 133
Diese schönen Gliedermassen 206
Dieses ist Amerika! 253
Die Wälder und Felder grünen 17
Die Welt ist dumm, die Welt ist blind 47
Die Welt ist so schön und der Himmel so blau 57
Doch die Kastraten klagten 146
Du bist wie eine Blume 122
Du bleibest mir treu am längsten 55
Du hast Diamanten und Perlen 130
Du liebst mich nicht, du liebst mich nicht 45
Du liegst mir so gern im Arme 213

Du schicktest mit dem Flammenschwert   242
Du schönes Fischermädchen   92
Du sollst mich liebend umschliessen   45
Du warst ein blondes Jungfräulein, so artig   20

Ein Fichtenbaum steht einsam   58
Eingehüllt in graue Wolken   94
Ein Jüngling liebt ein Mädchen   63
Einsam klag' ich meine Leiden   7
Entflieh mit mir und sei mein Weib   224
Er ist so herzbeweglich   219
Es blasen die blauen Husaren   142
Es drängt die Not, es läuten die Glocken   187
Es erklingen alle Bäume   185
Es fällt ein Stern herunter   77
Es fiel ein Reif in der Frühlingsnacht   225
Es geht zu End', es ist kein Zweifel   271
Es kommt der Tod; jetzt will ich sagen   272
Es kommt zu spät, was du mir lächelst   209
Es läuft dahin die Barke   219
Es leuchtet meine Liebe   68
Es liegt der heisse Sommer   69
Es schauen die Blumen alle   65
Es stehen unbeweglich   42
Es träumte mir von einer Sommernacht   274
Es treibt mich hin, es treibt mich her!   10
Es war ein alter König   191
Es war mal ein Ritter, trübselig und stumm   36

Freundschaft, Liebe, Stein der Weisen   64
Fürchte nichts, geliebte Seele   203

Gaben mir Rat und gute Lehren   132
Geh nicht durch die böse Strasse   208
Gekommen ist der Maie   183
Geleert hab' ich nach Herzenswunsch   272
Gesanglos war ich und beklommen   218
Gewiss, gewiss, der Rat war gut   20

Habe auch in jungen Jahren   143

Habe mich mit Liebesreden 128
Hast du die Lippen mir wund geküsst 139
"Hat sie sich denn nie geäussert" 112
Heller wird es schon im Osten 173
Herr Peter und Bender sassen beim Wein 233
Herz, mein Herz, sei nicht beklommen 121
Himmlisch war's, wenn ich bezwang 144
Hör' ich das Liedchen klingen 64
Hörst du nicht die fernen Töne 32

Ich bin die Prinzessin Ilse 174
Ich bin nun fünfunddreissig Jahr' alt 221
Ich bin's gewohnt den Kopf recht hoch zu tragen 34
Ich dacht' an sie den ganzen Tag 18
Ich glaub' nicht an den Himmel 54
Ich grolle nicht, und wenn das Herz auch bricht 49
Ich hab' dich geliebet und liebe dich noch! 67
Ich habe gerochen alle Gerüche 258
Ich hab' euch im besten Juli verlassen 137
Ich hab' im Traum geweinet 74
Ich hab' mir lang den Kopf zerbrochen 128
Ich halte ihr die Augen zu 201
Ich hatte einst ein schönes Vaterland 222
Ich kann es nicht vergessen 60
Ich liebe solche weisse Glieder 215
Ich mache die kleinen Lieder 270
Ich rief den Teufel und er kam 113
Ich stand in dunkeln Träumen 105
Ich steh' auf des Berges Spitze 72
Ich trat in jene Hallen 102
Ich unglücksel'ger Atlas! Eine Welt 106
Ich wandelte unter den Bäumen 11
Ich wandle unter Blumen 190
Ich war, o Lamm, als Hirt bestellt 282
Ich weiss eine alte Kunde 31
Ich weiss nicht, was soll es bedeuten 85
Ich will meine Seele tauchen 42
Ich wollte bei dir weilen 126
Ich wollte, meine Lieder 12
Ich wollt' meine Schmerzen ergössen sich 129

Ihr Lieder! Ihr meine guten Lieder! *176*
Im Anfang war die Nachtigall *186*
Im düstern Auge keine Träne *247*
Im nächt'gen Traum hab' ich mich selbst geschaut *6*
Im Rhein, im schönen Strome *44*
Im Traum sah ich die Geliebte *118*
Im Traum sah ich ein Männchen, klein und putzig *6*
Im Walde wandl' ich und weine *88*
Im Wald, in der Köhlerhütte sitzt *250*
Im wunderschönen Monat Mai *39*
In dem abendlichen Garten *153*
In den Küssen, welche Lüge *140*
In der Hand die kleine Lampe *233*
"In meiner Brust, da sitzt ein Weh" *23*
In meiner Erinn'rung erblühen *192*
In mein gar zu dunkles Leben *84*
In welche soll ich mich verlieben *210*

Ja, du bist elend, und ich grolle nicht *49*
Ja, freilich, du bist mein Ideal *204*
Ja, Freund, hier Unter den Linden *145*
Jugend, die mir täglich schwindet *212*
Jüngstens träumte mir: Spazieren *216*

Kaum sahen wir uns, und an Augen und Stimme *147*
Keine Messe wird man singen *283*
Kind! Es wäre dein Verderben *122*
König ist der Hirtenknabe *172*

Lehn deine Wang' an meine Wang' *41*
Leise zieht durch mein Gemüt *184*
Lieb Liebchen, leg's Händchen aufs Herze mein *12*
Liebste, sollst mir heute sagen *47*

Mädchen mit dem roten Mündchen *123*
Mag da draussen Schnee sich türmen *124*
Manch' Bild vergessener Zeiten *62*
Man glaubt, dass ich mich gräme *110*
Meine gute, liebe Frau *281*
Meine Qual und meine Klagen *36*

Meiner goldgelockten Schönen   231
Mein Herz, mein Herz ist traurig   86
Mein Kind, wir waren Kinder   115
Mein Knecht! Steh auf und sattle schnell   25
Mein Liebchen, wir sassen beisammen   66
Mein süsses Lieb, wenn du im Grab   57
Mein Wagen rollet langsam   73
Mensch, verspotte nicht den Teufel   114
Mir träumte: Traurig schaute der Mond   107
Mir träumte von einem Königskind   65
Mir träumte wieder der alte Traum   72
Mir träumt: Ich bin der liebe Gott   134
Mit deinen blauen Augen   189
Mit Rosen, Zypressen und Flittergold   15
Morgens send' ich dir die Veilchen   192
Morgens steh' ich auf und frage   9

Nach Frankreich zogen zwei Grenadier'   26
Nacht lag auf meinen Augen   80
Nacht liegt auf den fremden Wegen   150
Nicht mehr barfuss sollst du traben   244
Nun ist es Zeit, dass ich mit Verstand   120

O Deutschland, meine ferne Liebe   229
O, mein gnädiges Fräulein, erlaubt   132
O schwöre nicht und küsse nur   46

Philister im Sonntagsröcklein   61

Sag mir wer einst die Uhren erfund   190
"Sag, wo ist dein schönes Liebchen"   152
Saphire sind die Augen dein   127
Schaff mich nicht ab, wenn auch den Durst   205
Schattenküsse, Schattenliebe   197
Schlage die Trommel und fürchte dich nicht   240
Schöne, helle, goldne Sterne   58
Schöne Wiege meiner Leiden   13
Schöne, wirtschaftliche Dame   149
Schwarze Röcke, seidne Strümpfe   162
Sei mir gegrüsst, du grosse   101

Seit die Liebste war entfernt   59
Selten habt ihr mich verstanden   146
Sie haben dir viel erzählet   52
Sie haben heut' Abend Gesellschaft   129
Sie haben mich gequälet   69
Sie hatten sich beide so herzlich lieb   226
Sie küssten mich mit ihren falschen Lippen   267
Sie liebten sich beide, doch keiner   112
Sie sassen und tranken am Teetisch   70
So hast du ganz und gar vergessen   50
Solche Bücher lässt du drucken!   241
So wandl' ich wieder den alten Weg   102
Spätherbstnebel, kalte Träume   194
Steht ein Baum im schönen Garten   207
Sterne mit den goldnen Füsschen   193
Sternlos und kalt ist die Nacht   179
Still ist die Nacht, es ruhen die Gassen   103
Still versteckt der Mond sich draussen   168

Täglich ging die wunderschöne   252
Tannenbaum, mit grünen Fingern   165
"Teurer Freund, du bist verliebt"   126
Teurer Freund! Was soll es nützen   119

Überall, wo du auch wandelst   208
Über die Berge steigt schon die Sonne   148
Und als ich euch meine Schmerzen geklagt   113
Und als ich so lange, so lange gesäumt   56
Und bist du erst mein ehlich Weib   140
Und die Husaren lieb' ich sehr   265
Und wüssten's die Blumen, die kleinen   51
Unser Grab erwärmt der Ruhm   269
Unsre Seelen bleiben freilich   214

Vergiftet sind meine Lieder   71
Verlor'ner Posten in dem Freiheitskriege   261
Verriet mein blasses Angesicht   125
Verstummt sind Pauken, Posaunen und Zinken   260
Von Harburg fuhr ich in einer Stund'   254
Von schönen Lippen fortgedrängt, getrieben   136

Während ich nach andrer Leute   203
Wahrhaftig wir beide bilden   280
Wandl' ich in dem Wald des Abends   195
Warum sind denn die Rosen so blass   51
Was treibt dich umher in der Frühlingsnacht   189
Was will die einsame Träne   107
Wenn der Frühling kommt mit dem Sonnenschein   34
Wenn ich an deinem Hause   98
Wenn ich auf dem Lager liege   123
Wenn ich bei meiner Liebsten bin   9
Wenn ich, beseligt von schönen Küssen   202
Wenn ich in deine Augen seh'   40
Wenn junge Herzen brechen   16
Wenn man an dir Verrat geübt   257
Wenn zwei von einander scheiden   70
Werdet nur nicht ungeduldig   120
Wer zum erstenmale liebt   131
Wie der Mond sich leuchtend dränget   117
Wie die Wellenschaumgeborene   48
Wie dunkle Träume stehen   138
Wie entwickeln sich doch schnelle   200
Wie kannst du ruhig schlafen   104
Wie langsam kriechet sie dahin   268
Wie neubegierig die Möwe   196
Wie rasch du auch vorüberschrittest   199
Wie schändlich du gehandelt   199
Wir fuhren allein im Dunkeln   137
Wir haben viel für einander gefühlt   53
Wir müssen zugleich uns betrüben   248
Wir sassen am Fischerhause   91
Wir standen an der Strasseneck'   205
Wohl unter der Linde erklingt die Musik   236
Wo ich bin, mich rings umdunkelt   80
Wo wird einst des Wandermüden   284

Zu dem Wettgesange schreiten   30
Zu der Lauheit und der Flauheit   131
Zu fragmentarisch ist Welt und Leben   128
Zu Halle auf dem Markt   148